Church
History
THE FIRST CENTURY

RICK JOYNER

MorningStar Publications
A DIVISION OF MORNINGSTAR FELLOWSHIP CHURCH
375 Star Light Drive, Fort Mill, SC 29715

Church History: The First Century
by Rick Joyner
Copyright © 2009

Distributed by MorningStar Publications, Inc., a division of MorningStar
Fellowship Church, 375 Star Light Drive, Fort Mill, SC 29715

International Standard Book Number: 978-1-60708-285-9; 1-60708-
285-3

MorningStar's website: www.MorningStarMinistries.org
For information call 1-800-542-0278.

Cover design by Kevin Lepp
Book layout by Dana Zondory

TABLE OF CONTENTS

Chapter One
THE REASON FOR THE QUEST 5

Chapter Two
THE BEGINNING 27

Chapter Three
CREATING THE NEW CREATION 41

Chapter Four
THE GREAT COMMISSION 55

Chapter Five
MAKING DISCIPLES 69

Chapter Six
THE FOUNDATION OF APOSTLES 75

Chapter Seven
TESTING APOSTLES 81

Chapter Eight
THE FOUNDATION OF PROPHETS 93

Chapter Nine
THE LIFE OF THE EARLY CHURCH........103

Chapter Ten
WAR OF THE SOUL 117

Chapter Eleven
JEWISH ROOTS AND GENTILE BRANCHES..131

Chapter Twelve
THE LAW PROPHESIED.................147

Chapter Thirteen
EARLY CHURCH GOVERNMENT 159

Chapter Fourteen
WOMEN IN THE EARLY CHURCH 183

Chapter Fifteen
PERSECUTION AND PERSEVERANCE 199

CHAPTER ONE
THE REASON
FOR THE QUEST

With the present and increasingly desperate problems facing the world and the church, an understanding of history may not seem to be the most pressing need we have today. However, in church history we can find the causes or reasons, as well as the solutions for many of these crises. In some form, the world and the church have faced many crises before, even if on a smaller scale, but that scale can make it far easier to understand them. In church history, we can find the answers to not only our current crises, but also to our future ones as well. If we had known history, we would not be in many of these crises now. It is a well-proven truth: "Those who do not know history are doomed to repeat it." The reverse is also true—by understanding our history, we can avoid many mistakes we would otherwise make.

I have an international reputation as a prophetic teacher. I have a special love for the prophetic gifts that the Lord gave to His church and for prophetic people. I also love history because I was shown early in my Christian walk that I could only be trusted with prophetic vision to the degree that I was moored to sound biblical doctrine and to understanding history.

The biblical prophets all seemed to have an expansive understanding of their history. They often used illustrations from that history for illuminating their visions of current events and the future, which likewise implied that those whom they were speaking to had an understanding of their history. This was because the Lord had commanded His people to recount their history to each generation. It is apparent from the writings of the New Testament and the early church fathers that this was also a discipline in the early church. However, this is actually rare in the church today. To use some of the most clear, powerful, and practical examples that history gives us, we have to teach history first.

The lack of understanding church history is no doubt one of the greatest weaknesses of the modern church. These weaknesses include such things as distorted theology, a shallow and misguided eschatology, church governments that cannot govern, and the repeated devotion to practices that keep the church distracted from its primary mandate. This ignorance also contributes to the poor ways that the church often relates to the world, the way Christians relate to other Christians, and even the way we relate to the Lord.

There are probably thousands of books being written on prophecy for every one that is written on church history, and yet an understanding of our history is required to understand biblical prophecies, which, as we will see, the Scriptures make clear. Not understanding our history is a root of the many conflicts and contradictions found in most books and teachings on prophecy and eschatology. We must understand history if we are going to understand our own times or the future.

THE HONOR AMONG PROPHETS

Only one of the Ten Commandments had a promise with it: **"Honor your father and your mother, that your days may be prolonged in the land which the Lord your God gives you" (Exodus 20:12)**. This promise is repeated in the New Testament (see Ephesians 6:2), declaring that our own spiritual longevity will be determined by the humility with which we honor those who went before us, who made our way straighter, and who spiritually gave birth to us. The pride of new spiritual generations who think that they are better than those who preceded them is a stumbling block, which has tripped almost every spiritual generation to date. Studying church history has a way of humbling us and is essential for spiritual health.

Honoring those who came before us is also essential for being trusted with the spiritual authority that we will need to accomplish our own mandates from the Lord. This is why Jesus submitted to the baptism of John and why, when Jesus was asked by what authority He did His works, He pointed to the baptism of John. John the Baptist was the last of an order—all of whom had prepared the way for the Lord. He was there to point to Jesus, declaring that He was indeed the One the prophets had all spoken of from the beginning. To fulfill all righteousness, Jesus honored John. This is an example for us too—that we need to be baptized in the teachings of those who have gone before us to prepare our way and make it straighter.

When we examine the mistakes of previous generations, it is not to dishonor them. Instead, just as the Scriptures are straightforward about the flaws or mistakes of even its greatest heroes, for the sake of those who will read and learn from them, we must do the same. Some of the greatest heroes in Scripture and church history also made some of the greatest mistakes. Some seemingly opened the windows of heaven and then turned around and opened a gate of hell. We must understand these so that we can open the windows of heaven, but not keep opening the gates of hell. The gates of hell are the openings that the enemy has used to gain entry into this world and the church to do his deadly work. The church has the authority to shut these gates, and at times she has used it with spectacular results. We are in increasingly desperate need of this in our own times. The historical examples of these can be a great motivation to rise up and use the authority we have been given.

In the last decade, it seems that a love for history and an understanding of the value of its lessons has been growing in the church. This is most encouraging, and we can expect this stronger link to our past to enable the Lord to trust us with more authority. It was no accident that it was at the Lord's baptism by John that the Holy Spirit descended upon Him and stayed. The Holy Spirit will bless many things, and visit some, but we are called to be the place where He can stay. In church history, we see many movements that were blessed and some that seemed to be genuine visitations of the Lord, but since the first century, there does not seem to have been a place for Him to remain. This should be our ultimate quest—to be His dwelling place.

Like the biblical prophets, it is apparent that the depth and quality of our prophetic perspectives will be determined to a high degree by our accurate and expansive knowledge of history. The height to which the Lord will take us to view the future is determined by how rooted and grounded we are, as well as how humble we are in being teachable by those who have gone before us. The span of our worldviews that we gain by understanding and interpreting history enables us to see further and with greater clarity into our own times, as well as the future.

The Mother Lode

If we knew the mother lode (the greatest vein of gold) was on our own property, we would be foolish to just leave it buried. Truth is much more valuable than gold or any other treasure, and God's truth trumps all other knowledge many times over. How can we just let our Bibles sit without mining the great treasure in them every day? It is a foolishness we will all regret on Judgment Day. Let us resolve now to use the strength and wisdom that we have to mine this great treasure and be good custodians of it.

What makes something a treasure is that it is either rare or hard to find. I have been an avid reader since I was very young and have found many treasures in the classics and the great books of our own times, but there is something far more valuable about the treasures of history. Maybe this is why antiques are more valuable than something that is just built—there is something about the treasures of age that makes them even more valuable. We will find treasures of wisdom and knowledge in history that will at times make current knowledge and wisdom seem shallow. However, the greatest treasures of all come from combining the two. We do not want to learn from the past just to learn from the past, but we want to see the lessons applied in our own times.

At times, this quest for the treasures of history will be like an adventure that keeps us on the edge of our seats. At times, it can seem boring because we must dig so deeply in one place before we get to the good stuff. This is even more difficult for a modern soul because we have been so conditioned by convenience and the immediate gratification of our desires. Look at the difference between modern sitcoms and those made just a few decades ago. In a comedy sitcom now, every statement must get a chuckle. Even if you begin watching in the middle of the show, it will still bring laughs because there is seldom a storyline, or if there is one, it is not essential to understand in order to be entertained. However, in watching early sitcoms, the whole program might build up to just one punch line at the end. You actually had to concentrate to get it, and once you did, the result was not just a chuckle, but you would laugh until you lost your breath. Not only would everyone be talking about the program the next day, but it would be remembered for a long time because it was so much deeper than what we watch today.

Many shallow treasures in history can be found fast and cheaply. To me, these are like the modern sitcoms, which do have some value. However, if you want the real treasures that will have a deep and lasting impact, it will take some patience and concentration to get them. I can assure you of this—they will be worth the search.

It is important to understand why the Lord gave us the written Word, but it is also important to have teachers and preachers so we can hear His Word. There is a difference in power to the Word that goes into us through the eye gate and the one that goes in through our ears, but they are both important. I can usually tell when someone loves the spoken word and listens to many teaching CDs or DVDs, because of the freshness and vibrancy in his or her spiritual life. I can also tell those who love to read by the depth in their life. Of course, we should have both—a love for preaching and teaching and a love for reading. Those who do will have freshness and depth in their lives.

Likewise, silver and gold go together. Silver is more common, but gold is more valuable because it is less common. We are told in Proverbs 25:11, the word spoken in good timing and proper circumstances is like **"apples of gold in settings of silver."** Therefore, I seek to write in a way so that every sentence has content and purpose, with valuable thoughts in each one, but also to build toward deeper insight. We need both.

If general knowledge must be covered at times to lay a foundation for understanding so we can develop a deeper insight, even when it is a bit tedious, I am confident you will quickly learn that the treasure is well worth the time and effort. You must think of yourself as a treasure hunter, a modern Indiana Jones. The excitement of the adventure is for the purpose of holding the treasure in your hands at the end of it. The journey can in itself be fulfilling, but it is actually about the treasure.

As you read this, I will try to be like a guide who is taking you to the great places I've found. If something stirs your heart to wander off in a certain direction on your own, to seek treasures that I may have missed, please take your liberty. In fact, I hope you are moved to do this at times. I will freely give you everything it has taken me decades to find, but your most valuable treasures will be the ones you uncover yourself. Therefore, one goal that I have is not just to give you treasure, but to make you a treasure hunter who is in relentless pursuit of the greatest treasure of all—God's truth.

I have lived a very blessed life in which I have been able to accomplish almost everything I really wanted to do, but one of the most rewarding has been the study of history. I have found God there, and He is the greatest of all treasures. We have had great fellowship studying these amazing human stories. However, it is obvious that this is an incomplete story. The chapter we are here to participate in should be better because of the lessons studied and learned from the past. The greatest result of studying history is that it helps us to make history ourselves and that this history will be good.

Our Mandate

The greatest purpose of what will be the last and greatest generation is to prepare the way for the Lord. We are told in Isaiah 40 that we prepare the way for the Lord by building this highway and making it level and straight. Church history has been more like a roller coaster. Understanding the cause of the violent ups and downs as well as the twists and turns can help us to be a part of making the final chapter of church history the glorious highway as prophesied in Isaiah 40—bringing the mountains and hills down, raising up the low places, and making the crooked paths straight.

The church at the end of the age is destined to be the greatest of all societies and will prepare the way for the coming kingdom of God by manifesting it in the middle of a crumbling world. Again, at the end of the church age, we are assured by Scripture that the nations will come to this highway, which is God's "higher-way" and will begin making their way to His kingdom. Our purpose is to build our part of this highway and direct the nations to it.

By illuminating the traps, mistakes, and "box canyons" that are on the path, our pace toward the goal can be greatly accelerated. Church history beautifully marks all of these so that we can avoid them without wasting so much time and energy. Those who are humble and diligent enough to learn these lessons will likely be the last generation of this great age because they will be able to finish the work.

Even though it may not seem like it, as our knowledge is elevated to see the bigger picture of God's plan. We will begin to see that the many different movements and denominations are all working on the same highway, even if at this time they are still too far apart to see each other. The exhortation in Isaiah 40 is to make the highway straight and level. That simply cannot be done without the knowledge acquired by those who have gone before us. It also has to be our desire to do it for future generations if the Lord tarries. What made John the Baptist "the greatest man ever born of woman" (see Matthew 11:11), according to Jesus, was that his whole devotion was to prepare the way for the One who was to come after him.

Church history is also a window into understanding all of human history. Through this we will see over and over how what is released in the heavens, the spiritual realm, is released on earth, both for good and evil. The church in its history has been a source of some of the greatest oppression, but it has also been the source of the greatest freedom movements, including the birthplace of modern democracy.

Israel's history has been described as an endless cycle of blessing, backsliding, judgment, repentance, then blessing again, backsliding again, and so on. The same could be said of church history. Einstein described insanity as doing the same thing over and over and expecting different results. By this definition, there has been much insanity in church history, and seeing it can help us break this cycle. The generation that breaks this cycle and remains faithful to the Lord will likely be the last generation of the church age and the ones that "make straight the way of the Lord."

My intent is not to make the history of the church look good or bad, but to be accurate in order to learn the lessons. Not knowing our history is not the cause of all of our problems, and knowing church history will not be the answer to all of them, nor will it make us perfect Christians. However, it will illuminate the cause of some of our worst and continuing mistakes and help us to avoid some of the traps that almost every succeeding generation has fallen into.

In church history, we will also find some of the greatest, most heroic acts in human history, which are a part of our heritage that we must learn from. Battles against some of the greatest darkness of our times have been fought before and won. They can be won again even more easily if we learn from these examples.

Overall, church history is the most compelling, inter-esting, and instructive of all human stories. Nothing else has such drama, tragedy, or comedy over such a long span of time. It crosses both cultures and eras and finds its way into the beginning of almost every human endeavor. In it you see the best and worst of human character, the worst human mistakes and the greatest triumphs. This history can therefore give us great insights into human nature, but even more important is the way it is also an expanding and confirming revelation of the Divine nature. After all, history comes from the words *"His—story."* For this reason, there may not be a more purposeful, interesting, or challenging study than that of church history.

As we understand this history, we will grow in faith and knowledge of our own purpose in these times because we will see more clearly the unfolding plan of God working. We cannot truly know where we are if we do not know where we are going and where we have been. A map is useless if we do not know where we are on the map. Knowledge of church history can give us this point of reference with great clarity and confidence.

As we study our history, at times it will become more apparent why many blame the church for the greatest darkness and evil perpetrated on man. There have been times when it was the source of these. Seeing this can help us to have a healthy empathy for many who are so resistant to the gospel and the church. This should help us to also better reach them as we come with a bit more humility and understanding, which means to "stand under" their situation.

However, true humility does not mean that we cannot be bold with our message. It is not the church that we are called to preach, but Christ, and there can be no flaw found in Him. He is the answer to every human problem, and as the biblical prophecies declare, Christ manifested through His church at the end of this age will not only bring about the greatest society the world has ever seen, but it will be the only refuge from the great time of trouble the world has brought upon itself.

At that time, the church will actually be more than a refuge—it will be a gateway to the kingdom, which is what we must now get ready for. As we do, we should understand that a number of times in the past, the church has sought to do this with some bad results. Because of this, many Christians have shied completely away from this mandate and have even changed their theology to accommodate this abdication. That is not the right answer. As we will see, some of the worst doctrines ever perpetrated upon the church were born out of the disappointment from mistakes and failures of the church, rather than the Scriptures.

Understanding how mistakes are made can help us to fulfill the biblical mandate to be what we are called to be without making the same mistakes. We should also consider that because a matter was tried and failed, the failure may not have been in what was tried but rather who was trying it, the timing, or both. Therefore, it is not enough to just know history to avoid repeating it, but we need to seek understanding of it through a wise and biblical evaluation.

Even with some of the mistakes made by Christians in the past, we will see why the church must also be credited with the greatest elevation and civilization of man. The church has been the greatest source of this during this age. Almost all (if not all) of the concepts that we consider "civilized behavior" today were established by the church. Just about every field of art, science, economic prosperity, and culture was born and nurtured in the church. Many of these later became rebellious children, but some of these wayward children in the sciences are also starting to drift back to their faith roots. Like the father of the prodigal son, the church must be ready to embrace them. We can embrace them in humility because the church has been a prodigal parent in many ways, running from its responsibility to its children, which could have prevented them from straying.

We may all have much repenting to do, but we also have much work to do to finish this story in the greatest of all triumphs that it will be. As the biblical prophecies make clear, the nations will be streaming to the city of God at the end of the story. It is now time to prepare for this, but a true understanding of this future must be built on a solid foundation of understanding our past.

THIS PERSPECTIVE

This is the first part of a general and basic study of church history that has a specific purpose—to highlight and learn from the great lessons of our history. Therefore, this narrative will not always flow in a linear path, but at times it will follow a theme in pursuit of its lessons. It is not intended to be only a narrative of dates, events, and people, but my basic goal is a search for relevant understanding, which will require us to sometimes jump around a bit through both time and places. I am especially seeking to highlight the important lessons that can be useful to us today.

I will also focus on the parts of this history that fulfill biblical prophecy because these are crucial for us to understand if we are to be prepared for the times. As events are unfolding at an increasingly fast pace, we need to get right to the point in our studies, and I will not take the time with some details that I would have otherwise.

Church history, or any history, is not a straight or narrow path, but it is more like a very broad and deep territory. Any history written will therefore be, to some degree, like one man's account of crossing a vast land, when if he had crossed on a different side than where he did, he might be telling a very different story. I have read histories from the Catholic perspective, the Reformation perspective, and from the perspectives of various other movements, and even one from the home church movement. At times, I wondered if I was reading about the same planet, much less the same period of time. I think there can be merit to each of these perspectives, but we do all see in part and know in part, so the best I am going to be able to present is only part of the picture. This should always be kept in mind.

If my studies had taken a different path, my perspective might be different, but this is not to imply that what I have written is not accurate. So much happened in each period that it would take a large library of books to cover it all in the kind of depth it deserves. There are many worthy events and people to research through history, and one of the most difficult things is to keep moving and not stop in one period and camp there. So if this study seems to be a superficial account, it is because it cannot be otherwise, and neither could any other history. However, that does not mean the accounts cannot still be illuminating.

Next to the Holy Spirit, the Bible is without question the greatest treasure that has been given to us. It is basically a history book of the greatest history of all—God's interaction with mankind. However, God is not an Author who wrote just one book and then retired. He has been active in the affairs of men from the beginning. Though this is not to in any way imply that the canon Scripture is incomplete, His actions throughout church history illuminate and establish the teachings of Scripture, fulfilling its prophecies with such stunning accuracy that it gives us even more confidence and boldness to walk this path we are on. No other entity has such foundations as the church.

Some metaphors used in Scripture to describe the church are that she is a building, a field, a bride, and an army. In church history, we can see all of these aspects, how the emphasis of one could bring great blessing, and the overemphasis of another could bring great tragedy. The generation that has the humility to honor their fathers and mothers in the faith by learning from them will be able to walk with much greater confidence in all that they are called to be, and they seem to be coming together now.

Even so, as a building, we will not build correctly unless we understand what we are built upon. Also, some parts to this building, even down to the foundation, must be reexamined before we build any higher. Many of the common beliefs that permeate Christianity are not even Christian in their origin or nature. As we examine some of the heresies and false doctrines that assaulted the church throughout the ages, we will be able to see more clearly their modern disguises and do some much needed repair on some of our theological and eschatological foundations.

A PERSONAL PERSPECTIVE

Because I believe very much in the biblical exhortation to **"know them which labor among you" (see I Thessalonians 5:12 KJV)**, you deserve to know my credentials for writing this. I am neither a trained theologian nor a historian. Even though I have studied this subject for nearly forty years, my study has not been as systematic or scientific as that of a professional, which is a weakness. I was simply on a quest to find the truth, and becoming a great lover of the church, I wanted to know how we arrived where we are, and what we could do to help her fulfill His purpose. Even so, I am a student of history more than a historian.

Also, because I was on a quest for understanding and was not thinking about writing a book about history when I was studying, I kept very poor notes on my findings. Therefore, I will make some statements that I cannot give references for and will use quotations at times without including the sources, because I simply wrote down the quotes and not the authors. I am now sorry that I did not do a better job of recording such things in my research, and I do not have the time to go back and correct this. In asking for your grace for this, I appeal to the New Testament, which often states "it is written" without telling us where.

Of course, I am not writing Scripture, and a more academic, scientific approach is not my purpose. My goal is to cover the parts of this history where I feel the great lessons are found, often passing over large periods of time where I did not find much. I think you will find this treatment interesting and useful, but it also has some weaknesses which you need to be aware of. There are certain weaknesses that I have from not being a trained theologian or historian, but there may also be some advantages that allow me to see things that the trained professionals might not see.

Even if we use the most academic and scientific approach to this study, with history we are looking through a glass darkly, almost to the same degree that we are when we seek to prophetically view the future. Most have played the game where one person whispers a story to the person beside him, and so forth, until it goes around the room, returning to the person who started it. By the time something is passed through just a couple of people, it is changed, and if it goes through more, it can become unrecognizable. History has been passed down to us, and it has been changed, sometimes a great deal. I have read more history books than anyone I know, yet I don't think I have ever read one that was truly objective or scientific in its approach. The more one claimed to be objective or scientific, the more it seemed to not be true.

For the most part, I was not consciously studying with partisan intent to establish a certain doctrine or position, but we all have our own points of view, or prejudices, and I certainly do not claim to be free of those. My most basic belief is that God was active in every generation, and I wanted to find and understand His actions to try and understand His ways better. I then wanted to understand how we arrived where we are and where we go from here.

I was given a commission to study church history as a mandate, which was essential for me to do what I am called to do. That mandate is to help prepare a generation who will preach the gospel of the kingdom throughout the whole world, building the last stages of that highway in Isaiah 40, which must be built to prepare the way for the Lord. Obviously, I am just one of many called to do this, but this is at least part of the drive behind all that I do and study. I did not study just looking for facts, but I studied looking for practical information that would help in our own times.

Regardless of how much prejudice we can find in any work, including history, each one can still be useful. The Holy Spirit can lead us to the truth, but we must depend on Him to do it. Where I may have added my own prejudices to this work, I trust that He will reveal them to those who need to see them. This is simply my perspective on the events and people that we will study, so I encourage you to **"test all things; hold fast what is good" (see I Thessalonians 5:21 NKJV).**

As I am also a builder, I had a goal while studying history to examine the foundations of the modern expression of Christianity to compare them to the original and to compare both of these to the biblical blueprints. This is not to attack, condemn, or be preoccupied with mistakes, but I do want to have a very clear understanding of what was built by God and what was built by man. This is with the hope that we will be able to abandon fruitless endeavors, correct the harmful ones, and concentrate on that which will advance the cause of Christ for our times. Our goal must be to see the city that God is building and to be a part of the building of that city, as He has so graciously invited us to do.

Sure Road to Success

As we proceed through history, it is obvious that many have been working on that highway in Isaiah 40 in virtually every generation. Even through the twists and ups and downs, many made heroic attempts to straighten the path for us. When we cruise down the freeway, we are not likely to be thinking of those who labored so hard to build it. The same is true of our spiritual highway. We are commanded to honor the previous laborers, and they deserve it.

I try to read the works of the great thinkers in many fields, but I have almost always been disappointed by what I found. It seems that most of these fields of knowledge are lacking a Newton or Einstein, a great genius in their field. When a science or field of knowledge have true geniuses to impact it, they elevate the baseline of knowledge so that those who sit at the table after them must rise to a very high standard. For some reason, the greatest geniuses tend to be found in physics, mathematics, and occasionally astronomy, and their brilliance has set a standard that the others have not been able to match. In reading these, you can sense the subtle chiding of physicists toward some other fields in science and knowledge for having such a low baseline of knowledge that their theories are immature, or even foolish. Such tends to bring disrepute on all science. My point here is that history is a field of knowledge that is crucial; yet few of the great thinkers have ever invested much in it. My prayer is that some who read this book will be inspired to elevate this field of knowledge in order for Christianity to come into its full and intended expression.

CHAPTER TWO

THE BEGINNING

**In the beginning God created the heavens
and the earth (Genesis 1:1).**

The first verse in the Bible is also the most important,
and the first four words are probably the most
important in the human language—**"In the beginning God."**
The understanding of this one verse is the foundation
upon which all truth is based. Before we can comprehend
the end of the age, or our present purposes, we must first
understand the beginning—that we are created by God
and for a purpose. This is the foundation upon which
everything else is built. We exist because of God; therefore,
we owe Him everything. He alone is worthy of our worship
and devotion.

It is not surprising that at the end of the age the most
pressing philosophical controversies still revolve around
our origin—at the end the greatest question is still the
beginning. This is understandable because when we answer
this question correctly, the answers to all other questions

are possible. If we answer it incorrectly, the door opens to almost every form of darkness and deception. So we want to start with what God did in the beginning and then proceed with what He has done since. In studying church history, we have to include much about what man did, but our focus will be to see and understand what God did and why.

The Human Delusion

In contrast to the simple truth that God created us, men have formulated many theories that they often assert with great confidence. Even the most brilliant and widely accepted of these theories are sometimes easily debunked with a child's logic, which is a revelation in itself. The devil must be laughing at the foolishness of what some are compelled to believe. The fact that men would even momentarily consider some of these theories, much less cling to them as truth, is begging for the intellectually honest to grasp the power of the simple and obvious truth that God created us. However, this truth comes with the ultimate obligation—when we accept this one fact, we will no longer have an excuse but will be compelled to serve Him.

This compulsion to serve our Creator seems to be an intellectual bondage, but to be free to think is actually the greatest liberation we can experience. Settling the ultimate question frees us to soar into the most exciting of all knowledge—the meaning of this universe. It does all have a meaning! The brilliance of its message eclipses all other knowledge. With this most basic question answered, our minds are free to soar the way that they were intended to.

However, we need to look briefly at how foolish some of men's theories are about how we arrived here. Without seeing God as the Creator, we are left to believe that all we know of our creation just happened by accident. As a physicist once said, the odds are better for a tornado to hit a junkyard and leave behind a perfectly formed Boeing 747 jet than to believe that the order and symmetry of this universe happened by accident. The odds are actually much better that an ape could throw a handful of chalk at a blackboard and the entire theory of relativity would be written in perfect cursive. Let's look at just a few of the basic facts of our existence. You may not see immediately what this has to do with church history, but eventually you will.

If we take the distance of the earth from the sun and reduce it to a scale of 100 miles, and if the earth's orbit was just the equivalent of one-eighth of an inch either closer or farther away from the sun over that 100-mile distance, we would either fry or freeze. When we consider the odds that the earth's orbit just happened to fall into the tiny slice of space where life could be supported, it is obviously great. Consider also how the earth tilts on its axis and spins at just the right speed to control the seasons, which are needed to keep one side from freezing over so that the earth does not wobble out of orbit. We are still far from being able to develop a computer that can even determine the odds of this happening like it did. One study acknowledged that they had not even been able to compute the odds that the gases found in our atmosphere would come together as they did in order to support life.

These are just a few of the thousands of combinations of events that had to take place for life to come forth on earth, each happening with perfect precision and timing. To believe that any one of these happened by accident would be amazing, but to believe that all of them happened the way that they did totally by chance should be grounds for determining insanity. However, many continue to tenaciously cling to such an unreasonable belief, causing my friends Norm Geisler and Frank Turek to write the book, *I Don't Have Enough Faith to Be an Atheist*. The foolishness of such incredible theories has caused an increasing number of top scientists to publicly admit: "We are not alone!"

Science has accomplished much for mankind. However, when theories such as evolution become so generally accepted and taught as fact, when the only evidence that man may have evolved from apes is that some still think this way, it reduces science to a mental level of thinking that obviously has not evolved very far. I am not trying to be mean or funny, but just like in the fairytale, someone needs to tell the emperor that those scientists don't have any clothes on. The discovery of DNA not only makes Darwinism obsolete, but makes it impossible. Darwin had some brilliant insights even if some of his conclusions went awry, but it is not likely that he would have come up with any of those conclusions if he had known about DNA.

It has been said that with the discovery of DNA, the Theory of Evolution was reduced to a level similar to someone finding a brand new Mercedes on the beach, with fuel in the tank, manuals in the glove compartment, keys in the ignition, and thinking that the ocean made it. The miracle of DNA found in a single cell is actually much greater than such a miracle as the ocean making a car. Now a good disciple of Darwin would contend that given millions of years, the ocean could have made this car, but I think we could give the ocean millions of years, and it would not even be able to make a single tire. Think about this: If the Theory of Evolution was true, there should be fossil evidence of it on practically every acre of ground on earth, but after more than two centuries, they are still searching for one single "missing link" and have not been able to find it. They claim to have found it many times, but every claim has fallen apart under honest evaluation.

God made us, and He had a plan. The ultimate elevation of the human spirit and mind is found in loving God. If we come to know Him, we cannot help but to love Him. As we are told in the Psalms, Romans, and other places in the Bible, the creation was given to reveal the Creator. He is clearly seen in the things that He made. His ways are revealed through the creation in such a way that Jon Amos Comenius, the man who is called "the father of modern education," declared, "Nature is God's second book."

Understanding this about creation is basic, but the church is a "new creation," a greater one, because it is both natural and spiritual and is therefore able to reveal the ways of God in a higher way than just the natural creation. Just grasping God's purpose for the church is elevating to the soul of man, compelling us to respond and try to fit into this highest purpose of God on the earth.

The conflict between light and darkness ultimately reveals the heart of man. We need to understand this. The church is called to be **"the pillar and support of the truth"** (see I Timothy 3:15), to stand against the darkness that seeks to destroy man. This is obviously the fulfillment of what Paul prophesied would come at the end of the age:

> **Now we request you, brethren, with regard to the coming of our Lord Jesus Christ and our gathering together to Him,**
>
> **that you may not be quickly shaken from your composure or be disturbed either by a spirit or a message or a letter as if from us, to the effect that the day of the Lord has come.**
>
> **Let no one in any way deceive you, for it will not come unless the apostasy comes first, and the man of lawlessness is revealed, the son of destruction,**
>
> **who opposes and exalts himself above every so-called god or object of worship, so that he takes his seat in the temple of God, displaying himself as being God.**
>
> **Do you not remember that while I was still with you, I was telling you these things?**

And you know what restrains him now, so that in his time he may be revealed.

For the mystery of lawlessness is already at work; only he who now restrains will do so until he is taken out of the way.

Then that lawless one will be revealed whom the Lord will slay with the breath of His mouth and bring to an end by the appearance of His coming;

that is, the one whose coming is in accord with the activity of Satan, with all power and signs and false wonders,

and with all the deception of wickedness for those who perish, because they did not receive the love of the truth so as to be saved.

For this reason God will send upon them a deluding influence so that they might believe what is false,

in order that they all may be judged who did not believe the truth, but took pleasure in wickedness.

But we should always give thanks to God for you, brethren beloved by the Lord, because God has chosen you from the beginning for salvation through sanctification by the Spirit and faith in the truth.

It was for this He called you through our gospel, that you may gain the glory of our Lord Jesus Christ.

So then, brethren, stand firm and hold to the traditions which you were taught, whether by word of mouth or by letter from us.

Now may our Lord Jesus Christ Himself and God our Father, who has loved us and given us eternal comfort and good hope by grace,

comfort and strengthen your hearts in every good work and word (II Thessalonians 2:1-17).

Just as the strength of a foundation will determine the magnitude of what can be built upon it, the depth to which we understand this one truth about our origin can determine the spiritual strength of our entire lives. When we understand that we had our beginning in God, that He made us for His purposes, we are therefore compelled to return to Him and serve Him in all that we do. The truth of our beginning is also the beginning of all truth. If He made us, we are His. When we know this, then His purpose and His plan must guide us.

THE BEGINNING AND THE END

If God made us, then we can no longer claim to be the center of this universe—He is. Jesus is the Alpha and the Omega, the Beginning and the End. He is *I Am.* All things will be summed up in Him. Just as every compass points to the magnetic north, He becomes the magnetic pole in our lives to which everything in us will begin to point. With this pole in our hearts, we have a basis for every decision—His will. He made us and we are His. All things came from Him, and all will return to Him. This is our destiny and the goal of our lives—to return to the One who made us, to love Him, and to serve Him.

It has been said that the most important step in any journey is the first one. How something begins is often the main determining factor in the quality of what is finished. Projects begun on an impulse are usually just as quickly and easily abandoned. For any significant project that is accomplished, the ability to plan with vision and strategy will be found as an obvious gift in its originator. Of course, the plan of God is the plan against which all other plans in heaven and earth will forever be measured. Our God planned from eternity, and as King Solomon understood, **"I know that everything God does will remain forever; there is nothing to add to it and there is nothing to take from it, for God has so worked that men should fear Him" (Ecclesiastes 3:14).** Therefore, it is to the degree that we are in harmony with His plan that our works will also remain.

The Second Beginning

This is the beginning of a study on church history, but our goal is not to know the church as much as it is to know the Creator of the church. When we address the beginning of the church, we are observing a second beginning with consequences no less profound than the first beginning in Genesis. The church does not just represent a new beginning for a few people who are so blessed to be chosen, but it represents a new beginning for the entire creation. That is why Paul asserted that "the whole creation groans and travails for the revealing of the sons of God" (see Romans 8:22).

It is no less important for us to recover the profound truth of Who created the church and why as it is for the rest of the creation to understand that God is its Creator. We may think this is a strange assertion since one must know God to even be a part of the church—that the church must "recover" this truth—but this has in fact been a confused issue from the first century. For this reason, much of the church was not created by God but by men. How can we distinguish between the two?

By not holding to this most basic issue, the church has often drifted far from its biblical moorings and has, at times, been the source of the greatest problems and delusions that has afflicted mankind. This is certainly one reason why the rest of mankind seems willing to embrace such ridiculous theories as evolution; they want just about anything that will help them stay away from what the church is teaching. This will not always be true. The Scriptures are clear that the church will recover a clear vision of her destiny and purpose at the end of this age, and that the nations will stream to her for truth (see Isaiah 2:1-4; 60:1-5).

If we are to know our purpose, we must recover the simple truths that God created us for His purpose and that He had a plan for us from the beginning. He will build His church according to His own plans. He wants to use us, but we must learn to follow Him in all things.

It is His house; He wants to use His own plans, and He will not live in anything else regardless of how wonderful we think it is.

FREEDOM TO FOLLOW

In His great wisdom, God set the ability to choose in the heart of man, the crowning glory of His creation. He created man to have a relationship with, but He knew that there could be no true relationship unless there was the freedom not to relate. Likewise, there could be no true obedience without the freedom not to obey. He did not put the Tree of the Knowledge of Good and Evil in the Garden in order to cause man to fall, but to allow man to prove his devotion and obedience by rejecting disobedience. Likewise, each man and woman on the earth has to choose whether to eat from this tree or not.

Even so, the Lord knew from the beginning that man would choose wrongly, eat of the Tree of Knowledge, and cause His creation to rebel against Him. He knew that when man fell, death and deception would mar the beauty of His creation. He made it anyway, knowing that the darkness would one day make His light even more glorious to those who would behold it. He loved His first creation, but He planned from the beginning to bring forth a new creation that would transcend the glory of the first one. He also determined that the glory of the second would result in the redemption of the first.

If we are to understand the history of the church, we must see it in the context of the whole plan of God. When we see His entire plan, we can understand why He would let the first creation fall into such depravity and then let the new creation follow the same course. Yes, the new creation also fell, following a remarkably similar path as the original creation. That is one reason why Jesus is referred to as **"the last Adam" (see I Corinthians 15:45).** His helpmate, the church, also partook of the forbidden fruit of the Tree of Knowledge, falling into terrible depravity.

However, unlike the first Adam, Jesus did not follow His bride. That is why He is the **"last Adam,"** not just the second one. He kept His place; He obeyed and never ate of the fruit of sin. That is why He can now redeem both the new and the original creation. He will restore His bride, and she will one day again be "without spot or wrinkle" (see Ephesians 5:27). Then, together, they will bring restoration to the rest of creation.

THE TWO WILL BECOME ONE

To understand the history of the new creation of God, we must also understand the first creation and the relation between the two. A reason for the first creation was to make it possible for the Lord to have a bride. She may have stumbled in many ways, but she will ultimately rise from the mire of sin and deception that has marked her life. She will ultimately prove her devotion, standing resolutely against the raging currents of the darkest of times to be faithful to Him. The first Eve chose to disobey even though she only knew light and truth and lived in a perfect paradise. The last Eve, the church, will live in the darkest of times and in the worst conditions but will choose to obey, proving herself worthy to reign with Him, even over the angels.

The new creation, the church, was so much in the heart of God from the beginning that we can see church history prophesied with astonishing clarity in the seven days of creation relayed in the first two chapters of Genesis. We can then see them repeated over and over throughout the Scriptures, each repetition providing different insights, but all of them confirming that the Lord foresaw all that would happen. When these prophecies become clear, they will release in us a profound confidence in the One we serve and in Whose plan we seek to walk in.

God has a glorious plan, and you are a part of it. He knew you from the beginning, and He is able to accomplish His purpose in your life. This is why we are looking back—to know more clearly why we are here now and where we are going. The quality of true prophetic vision will always be dependent upon the depth of our knowledge of the Scriptures and how they apply to the unfolding of God's plan through history.

THE LAST WILL BE FIRST

If you do not have knowledge of church history, you can read the creation story in Genesis from now until the end of time and not see how it prophesied that history. That is why Proverbs states repeatedly that knowledge comes before understanding. This is a basic quest of this study, to gain the knowledge that is required as a basis for understanding. Then knowledge and understanding become a basis for wisdom. This **"cord of three strands"** (**see Ecclesiastes 4:12**) will not be easily broken.

That is why Daniel was instructed to **"seal up the book until the end of time"** (**see Daniel 12:4**). There are many prophecies in Daniel, the Book of Revelation, and the rest of the Scriptures which simply could not be understood until the end and by the knowledge we have gained through our history. That these books are now being "opened" or understood is one of the sure signs that we have indeed come to the end of this age. It is one of the great paradoxes and glories of God's wisdom—that the end could not be understood without an understanding of the beginning. He is both the Alpha and the Omega. To know Him as He is, we must see Him as both, and we must understand His plan for both.

Many have come to understand a great deal about what the Lord has done. Others seem to know a lot about what He is going to do at the end. If we see Him as He is, we must see Him from the beginning to the end. Our reason for seeing either is to walk with Him today. If our knowledge of the past or the future does not translate into a closer relationship with Him now, then we are still trapped in the letter that kills.

Again, our goal for seeing Him more clearly in the past or the future is that we see Him more clearly today. This is why we will constantly seek to apply the lessons of history to the present in this study, and then we will use them for viewing the future.

CHAPTER THREE
CREATING THE NEW CREATION

Because beginnings are so crucial, as we look at the beginning of the new creation, we will be confronted by important truths to understand which much of the rest of our understanding will be based on. Digging a foundation for a building can be hard work, but it is necessary for the stability of the whole building, and therefore must be done carefully. We will look more at the time when the foundations of the church were being laid than any other period.

The beginning of both creations can be summed up in one word—Jesus. He is called **"the Beginning of the creation of God" (see Revelation 3:14)**, not because He Himself is created, but because the entire plan of creation began with Him. In fact, the Scriptures make it clear that Jesus is the Creator, as we see in the following texts:

In the beginning was the Word, and the Word was with God, and the Word was God.

The same was in the beginning with God.

> All things were made by Him; and without him was not anything made that was made (John 1:1-3 KJV).

> For by him were all things created, that are in heaven, and that are in earth, visible and invisible, whether they be thrones, or dominions, or principalities, or powers: all things were created by him, and for him:

> And he is before all things, and by him all things consist (Colossians 1:16-17 KJV).

Jesus is the reason for the creation, both the old and the new. This is the most important truth that we can understand, and it is the true revelation of what **"in the beginning God"** (**see Genesis 1:1**) means. Paul wrote to the Ephesians:

> Having made known unto us the mystery of his will, according to his good pleasure which he has purposed in himself:

> That in the dispensation of the fullness of times he might gather together in one all things in Christ, both which are in heaven, and which are on earth; even in him (Ephesians 1:9-10 KJV).

Jesus is everything that the Father loves, the desire of His heart. In everything that was created, He was looking for His Son, and He is looking for His Son in us. The goal of our lives is to be found in Him. The ultimate goal of the whole creation, the new and the old, the heavens and the earth, is to be summed up in Him. This is why it is so important that in the beginning we understand this one truth:

> **For no man can lay a foundation other than the one which is laid, which is Jesus Christ.**
>
> **Now if any man builds on the foundation with gold, silver, precious stones, wood, hay, straw,**
>
> **each man's work will become evident; for the day will show it, because it is to be revealed with fire, and the fire itself will test the quality of each man's work (I Corinthians 3:11-13).**

The church was originally conceived in the heart of the Father as a fitting bride for His Son, just as Eve was brought forth to be the perfect helpmate for the first Adam. However, the bride is for the Son, not the other way around. If we do not stay focused upon this ultimate purpose of the church, that we exist for Him, and that the goal of everything we do is to be joined to Him we will be continually distracted by the lesser purposes. When a lesser purpose of God starts to eclipse His ultimate purpose, the process of deception has begun.

We must not build upon truths, but rather upon the Truth Himself. We cannot build upon the gifts of God—neither natural or spiritual. We cannot try to build the church of God upon charismatic preachers, regardless of how true their preaching is or how great their gifts are. The true church will only be built upon the one Foundation, Jesus Christ Himself.

We should always ask this question: Why are people gathered to what we are building? Is it because they agree with our truths? Is it because of our dynamic ministries? Is it because of our facilities? Our music? Or is it because the Lord Jesus Himself is in our midst and we are all being joined to Him?

TRUE CHURCH LIFE

The reason that the church emerged in the Book of Acts was because the Lord was among them. They had encounters with Him every day. He was their message, and He did great works among them. It seems as if the Lord purposely chose leaders for His new church that absolutely no one would follow unless they were anointed with His presence.

The first-century church really had only one thing going for them—God. The Lord was with them. There was no other way to explain what happened. No one would follow fishermen, tax gatherers, and peasants who had proven that they were faithless and undependable, even deserting the Lord when He needed them the most. Unless the Lord was with them, the first leaders of the church had no hope of accomplishing their purpose of being used to build the church. The Lord had His first leaders in a place where they were completely dependent on Him to do the works. If the Lord did not show up, they were helpless. That is precisely the foundation that we must return to—**"in the beginning God"** (see Genesis 1:1).

The church began in such a way that this was an unquestionable reality. From that point on, the history of the church could be summed up this way: *after the beginning . . . man.* The new creation began with a close fellowship with God, walking with Him just as Adam and Eve did in the Garden. The church also chose to eat of the forbidden fruit. We began to look at ourselves and cover ourselves, while actually trying to hide from God.

WE MUST BE BORN AGAIN, AGAIN

It is now time for the church to be born again, again. We must return to our beginning. Many have been hearing this call for years but have often interpreted it that we need to return to the *way* the first-century church did things. Of course, there is a lot of merit to this, but more than that we need to return to the One who did the works. The Lord is going to insist on building His own house.

If the Lord showed up and began to do the building in most of our congregations, it would really mess up the program. One friend of mine used to begin his sermons with, "Well, if the Lord does not show up today, we have a pretty good program anyway." This was shocking to many people, but much more honest than what most of us do—claiming that what we do is God. We have become very skillful at keeping people entertained and occupied, believing that God is doing many things that He honestly would not touch. This could be what the Lord meant when He said:

> **My people have become lost sheep; their shepherds have led them astray. They have made them turn aside on the mountains; they have gone along from mountain to hill and have forgotten their resting place (Jeremiah 50:6).**

This is probably the most frequent way that the Lord's people have been led astray from the beginning—going from mountain to hill, from hype to hype, from one thing that pumps them up to the next. They always keep moving but are never being led to their resting place—a relationship to the Lord of the Sabbath Himself.

This is also a primary reason for the Laodicean lukewarmness that permeates so much of the church today. The people are simply weary from all of the hype and projects that are forced upon them that God is not in. They signed up for the Lord, but somehow all they ever get is us! We have tried to build the church on almost everything but the only Foundation that will ever work—the Lord Jesus Himself.

We see in Revelation 3:20 that the Lord is on the outside of most of our churches trying to get in. He is a gentleman and will not force Himself upon His bride. Building on the foundation of Jesus is much more than just teaching about Him. It is more than just inviting Him in; it is letting Him build the building.

In this day, when we have so much that will attract people, it is difficult to build something in utter dependence on God. During the Middle Ages, St. Francis was reported to have been walking with a friend who was pointing out the glories of their city cathedral to him. Observing the great treasures of the church, the friend remarked that the church could no longer say, "Silver and gold have I none," to which the leader replied, "And neither can we say, 'In the name of Jesus rise up and walk.'" Many great things have been done in the name of the Lord, but how many of them have actually been done by the Lord?

The Lord has blessed many great works and movements, and He has even occasionally visited a few with His manifest presence, but it does not seem that there has been a church since the first century about which it could be said that the Lord truly dwells with her. Is this not our quest, to find the city that God is building? One of the ultimate questions we need to ask concerning the church is this: "Where does God dwell?"

THE FOUNDATION OF PAUL

For the first one thousand years of church history, the institutional church which had evolved claimed to be seated upon the seat of Peter. Peter's ministry and message were the main focus of that time, and the church reflected it. Spectacular victories were followed by shocking errors. The Reformation actually began with a rediscovery of the Epistles of Paul, and since then, the main emphasis of the church has been the theology of Paul.

Paul was unquestionably one of the great builders of the New Testament church. It was his theology and revelation more than anyone's that set a true course for Christianity. Even so, Peter is not the foundation of the church, and neither is Paul—Jesus is. Since the Reformation, we have tended to use Paul to interpret Jesus, rather than the other way around. The foundations of Christian truth are the teachings of Jesus, not Paul, not Peter, and not anyone else.

This is not to in any way imply that Paul's Epistles do not deserve to be canon Scripture or that they are not pure Words from God. However, we will misinterpret them and misapply them if they are not rightly built upon the foundation of the teachings of Jesus. Likewise, the teachings of Jesus will be misinterpreted and misapplied if we try to view them through the teachings of anyone else, rather than as the foundation for all other understanding.

Paul's teachings made many great and insightful references to the kingdom of God, but they mostly dealt with the practical issues of the church and some basic issues of doctrine. The church is a part of the kingdom of God, but it is just a part. The Lord's teachings were devoted to the kingdom, and only made a few references to the church. Unless the church is viewed from this perspective, we will become church-centric rather than Christ-centric.

When the church becomes self-centered, she loses her ability to see the glory of the Lord and to be changed by that glory. She will also have a distorted view of the kingdom and, therefore, a distorted view of her relationship to the world that the kingdom is coming to.

THE ONE LOAF

Many think of the Gospels as the milk that we give to new believers, but when we mature, we go on to the apostolic Epistles. This is a terrible delusion. The greatest depth of revelation that we will ever find in the Bible is found in the Gospels. A depth of understanding is to be had in every parable and every miracle that few have even begun to fathom. John 6 is one of the pivotal chapters in the Bible, and I think it is one that is especially relevant to us now.

This chapter begins with a great multitude following Jesus because of the signs that they saw Him performing (verse 2). It was the time of the Passover, and since Jesus was the Passover Lamb sent from God, He would feed the people as a sign. One thing that is often overlooked is that signs point to something. Every miracle that Jesus did was a message. So Jesus fed the five thousand.

After the Lord had gone to the other side of the lake, the people found Him, and He rebuked them because they were not following Him for the signs but because of the food He had given to them (see verse 26). He then gave one of the most important teachings in the Scriptures, declaring that He Himself is the Bread which came down from heaven, and if we do not partake of Him, we will not have life. It then says, **"As a result of this many of His disciples withdrew and were not walking with Him anymore"** (verse 66).

Many other basic truths are in this chapter, but the main point is that many follow Him because of the miracles, and many more will follow Him for His provision. When it comes down to how many are following Him for who He is, there will not be many left.

If we want big crowds to follow our ministry, we can preach either signs and wonders or God's provision, and we will probably never be lacking for people. These things are not wrong; they are in fact great biblical truths, but when they become the reason that we are following Him, they become idols and a false foundation for faith. We want to preach signs and wonders and see God's provision, but above all else, we must know Him and be joined to Him.

Signs and wonders or God's provision are individual truths, but if they are what we are building on, the day will come when there will not be many left. The loaves that the Lord gave to the people were representative of individual truths. After the people ate of the loaves, what did they have left over? Fragments! Then Jesus explained to them that He is the one Loaf!

We must not continue trying to build the church on individual truths, but instead on a relationship with Jesus who is the Truth. Only then will we be able to partake of the individual truths and not have them divide us. Any truth that is taken in isolation from His living Person will be divisive, as the Scriptures themselves teach.

> **God, after He spoke long ago to the fathers in the prophets in many portions and in many ways,**
>
> **in these last days *has spoken to us in His Son*** (see Hebrews 1:1-2).
>
> **"You search the Scriptures because you think that in them you have eternal life; it is these that testify about Me"** (John 5:39).
>
> **For as many as are the promises of God, *IN HIM* they are yes** (see II Corinthians 1:20).

> **Now the promises were spoken to Abraham and to his seed.** *He does not say, "And to his seeds," as referring to many, but rather to one, "And to your seed," that is, CHRIST* **(Galatians 3:16).**

When we take the promises of God individually or apart from Him, and not in union with Him, even they can become idols to distract us from the Tree of Life Himself. None of the promises are made to us as individuals, or even as the church, but *"in Him."*

The Son of Man is still seeking a place to lay His head, a place where He can be the Head. When we devote ourselves to building a church that attracts God, instead of just something that will attract people, we will at least be starting in the right direction. This is our quest: to be a part of the church that has Christ as both the Foundation and the Head. Our goal is not just to establish men in authority, but to establish Christ as authority over men. We must preach the kingdom by exhibiting Jesus as the King.

THE FIRST STONE IN THE FOUNDATION

When Jesus was born, the only way He could be found was by revelation. The same is still true. In Matthew 16:13-18, we see the first stone laid in the foundation of the church and the way in which every subsequent stone must be laid:

> **Now when Jesus came into the district of Ceasarea Philippi, He was asking His disciples, "Who do people say that the Son of Man is?"**

51

And they said, "Some say John the Baptist; and others, Elijah; but still others, Jeremiah, or one of the prophets."

He said to them, *"But who do you say that I am?"*

Simon Peter answered, "You are the Christ, the Son of the living God."

And Jesus answered and said to him, "Blessed are you, Simon Barjona, *because flesh and blood did not reveal this to you, but My Father who is in heaven.*

"I also say to you that you are Peter, (a stone) and upon this rock (a large rock or bedrock) I will build My church; and the gates of Hades shall not overpower it."

The bedrock that the church is built upon is the revelation from the Father. It is not who men say that He is; we each must have our own revelation of Him. We must each have our own well that we drink the waters of Life from. Probably the main reason why Solomon fell after building the temple was that he only had his father's vision, and after he finished that work, he did not have a vision of his own. The strength of every congregation will be dependent upon how strong every individual's personal relationship to the Lord is.

Immediately after Peter expressed his revelation of who Jesus was, he was taken to the Mount of Transfiguration along with James and John. This was possibly the second most important revelation for those who would be the leaders of the church to have, and for us to have as well.

Six days later Jesus took with Him Peter and James and John his brother, and led them up on a high mountain by themselves.

And He was transfigured before them; and His face shone like the sun, and His garments became as white as light.

And behold, Moses and Elijah appeared to them, talking with Him.

Peter said to Jesus, "Lord, it is good for us to be here; if You wish, I will make three tabernacles here, one for You, and one for Moses, and one for Elijah."

While he was still speaking, a bright cloud overshadowed them, and behold, a voice out of the cloud said, "This is My beloved Son, with whom I am well-pleased; listen to Him!"

When the disciples heard this, they fell down to the ground and were terrified.

And Jesus came to them and touched them and said, "Get up, and do not be afraid."

And lifting up their eyes, they saw no one except Jesus Himself alone (Matthew 17:1-8).

The first thing that the disciples saw was the Lord glorified and Moses and Elijah speaking to Him. Moses and Elijah represented the Law and the Prophets, both of whom spoke of Him. However, the first response of Peter was to think about building something for this great revelation. Then the Father spoke: **"This is My beloved Son . . . listen to Him!"** Then they fell on their faces and were much afraid. They badly needed this rebuke, and so do we. The Lord does not want us to try to build on our revelations, not even our revelations of who He is. When a revelation comes, our first response must not be to build, but to keep listening—there is much more!

After this rebuke from the Father, they lifted up their eyes and **"saw no one except Jesus Himself alone."** That is the most important revelation that we can have. Until we see Him as the whole revelation, as the whole Loaf, as the whole purpose of God, we are not ready to build.

CHAPTER FOUR
THE GREAT COMMISSION

In the last chapter, we examined the foundation of the church as it was built upon the living relationship to Jesus Himself. Now we will look at the foundational message of the church and the manner in which the first-century church sought to present that message to the world and its impact. Our mandate is to proclaim this same message, which will not change until the end of this age, even if the method of its delivery can be, and is, modified at times to reach current generations.

A SENSE OF DESTINY

The life of the church which emerged in the Book of Acts was the result of one basic factor—the Lord was in their midst. They had encounters with Him day by day. He was their message, and He did great works among them. This is the most crucial element to the success of the church—God is with us.

The leaders of the church had begun their commission immediately after such great failures as denying the Lord and fleeing from Him while He was in His greatest time of need. It seems that the Lord purposely chose leaders for His new church that no one would follow unless these leaders were so anointed that the people would overlook their previous mistakes or flaws. The leaders had nothing going for them but the Lord, but He was all they needed. It remains the most important thing any Christian leader needs.

Many, if not most, of the great church leaders in history had major mistakes in their pasts, which seems to have been a necessary element to keep them humble and dependent on Him. Even today the oldest, wisest Christians will not trust people too much until "they have their limp," referring to the limp that Jacob got that allowed the Lord to change his name to Israel, which means "a prince with God." It is one thing to have authority or influence with men, which can be attained cheaply, but it can be altogether different to have authority with God. True leadership in the Lord is having authority with God, not just men. Just as Peter was elevated to give the message and to give birth to the church on the Day of Pentecost right after his most tragic mistake of denying the Lord, the Lord uses the humble, contrite, and the wise for the basis of true authority.

The first-century church existed only because of the Lord. It had no alternative plan, nothing else to fall back on. There was not an entertainment system to draw people to them, but rather the definite threat of persecution and even death. If the Lord ceased to dwell among them, they would certainly be scattered. But the Lord was among them, and He was the One doing the building. The Genesis of the "new creation" can only be explained in the same terms as the original creation—*"In the beginning—God."* He was among them, and He was the reason for their existence.

Even so, the church had a purpose that went beyond gathering—to experience the Lord each day. Before His ascension, the Lord had given them a commission, which has since been called "The Great Commission":

> **And Jesus came up and spoke to them, saying, "All authority has been given to Me in heaven and on earth.**
>
> **"Go therefore and make disciples of all the nations, baptizing them in the name of the Father and the Son and the Holy Spirit,**
>
> **"teaching them to observe all that I commanded you; and lo, I am with you always, even to the end of the age" (Matthew 28:18-20).**

The foundation of the Great Commission is that all authority has been given to Jesus in both heaven and earth. The Great Commission is essentially the proclamation of His authority. The message of the church was not the church. She was not sent forth to establish her own authority but to proclaim His. For the entire time that Jesus walked the earth, He only made a couple of brief references about the church. His message was much larger than the church; it was the kingdom of God. When the first-century church began to go forth with her message, it was not a message about herself, but about her King.

The apostolic burden was not to bring the church into a certain form, but to see Jesus formed within His people. There is a difference. One is Christ-centered; the other is man-centered. The more church-centric that the church became, the quicker she fell into the prophesied apostasy. As long as her message remained on Christ, she remained pure and on course. When building the church became primary, the church deviated from its course. Building the church is essential, but nothing should ever eclipse our devotion to proclaiming Christ and His kingdom.

This is not meant to in any way detract from the glory of the church. She is called to be the Bride of the Lamb. Her true destiny is glorious, beyond our present comprehension. However, we will never become who we are called to be by looking at ourselves. We will only be changed into who we are called to be as we behold His glory.

But we all, with unveiled face, beholding as in a mirror the glory of the Lord, are being transformed into the same image from glory to glory, just as from the Lord, the Spirit (II Corinthians 3:18).

The more focused we are on who we are, the less likely we are to fulfill our main purpose, which is to be like Him and to do the works that He did. One of the greatest distractions to come upon the church has been the *over-emphasis* of who we are in Christ, instead of who He is in us. It is important for us to know who we are called to be, but we will never be who we are called to be as long as that is our primary devotion.

The church became and remained what she had been called to be only as long as she remained faithful to the message of the kingdom of God. That message was, simply stated, that Jesus is the King. The apostolic burden was not just to get people into the church, but to see Jesus formed in His people and to see His name made a glory in the earth. That is why the Great Commission was not just to make converts, but to make *disciples.* The true disciples were those who were taught to observe *all* that Jesus had commanded.

Day after day the apostles taught what they had been commanded. This was as much a fulfilling of the Great Commission as it was the preaching of the gospel for the salvation of souls. Seeing so many being born again was wonderful, but when we are born we are just beginning our lives, and the same is true when we are born again. This is just the beginning of our journeys, not the end. The ultimate goal of the apostles was to see those who joined themselves to the Lord become like Him. Anything less than this is a diluting of the gospel message that we have been given.

We can never fulfill the Great Commission by just proclaiming Jesus as Savior; He must be Lord of all, or He is not Lord at all. If there is just one word that could sum up the essence of the Great Commission, it is the word *all.* Jesus had been given *all* authority in heaven and on earth. True disciples were taught to observe *all* that He had commanded them. This message was *all* encompassing to those who embraced it. Their faith was not just an appendage added to their lives that required them to go to some meetings. Knowing Jesus, following Him day by day in every place and in every situation, was fundamental to the life of the early church. He became *all* to them.

Jesus is the Way, the Truth, and the Life. We cannot truly know the Way and the Truth until He becomes our Life. The Way is not just believing a few fundamental truths about the Lord—the Way *is* the Lord. The Truth is not found by just agreeing with certain doctrines, even all Christian doctrines—the Truth is a Person who must be our whole Life. Only if we know Him as our Life do we really know the Way and the Truth.

WE MUST EAT THE WHOLE THING

Because the first members of the church were all Jews, they had a basic understanding of Jesus as the Passover Lamb of God. When the children of Israel were instructed to partake of the first Passover lamb, which was a type of Christ, so that the angel of death would pass over them, they were instructed to eat the whole lamb, including its head and entrails and not to leave any of it over until morning (see Exodus 12:7-10). This was a prophetic statement that if we are going to partake of the Passover Lamb of God, we cannot pick and choose which parts of Him we want, but we must be taught to do all that He commanded to be true disciples.

If we are going to partake of God's provision for us in His Son, we cannot say that we want His salvation but not His Lordship, His Holy Spirit, or the ministries that

He gave to the church so that she might "**grow up in *all* aspects into Him**" (**see Ephesians 4:15**). Until we are like Christ and do the works that He did, we have not been completed yet.

Paul wrote to the Corinthians that "**the testimony concerning Christ was confirmed in you, so that you are not lacking in *any* gift (see I Corinthians 1:6-7).** All of the ministries and gifts of the Spirit are but aspects of Christ that He demonstrated when He walked the earth in the flesh. They are demonstrated in the church because He still dwells among us by the Holy Spirit. The functioning of any ministry is actually the moving of Christ within our midst. If we limit any of the gifts or ministries, we are rejecting that aspect of Christ. If we are going to be *all* that we have been called to be, we must open our hearts to *all* of Him.

Therefore, the Great Commission cannot be fulfilled until all of the equipping ministries are working together. It may begin with an evangelist proclaiming the good news of salvation, but it must be followed up with the work of the other equipping ministries given to the church. Philip is the only example in Scripture of one who was a pure evangelist (see Acts 8:4-8). Philip needed others (Peter and John) to come and follow-up his ministry so that the converts were established in the Lord. The foundation was not laid until they were made disciples, not just converts.

In the New Testament narrative of the formation of the church, we see that those who were converted were added to the church. Today it is estimated by some of our greatest evangelists that only about 5 percent of those who "make decisions for Christ" are added to the church. We should be thankful for any who are brought in. However, can we really call this the fulfilling of the Great Commission if this is the percentage who go on to be a part of the church? What has caused this slide from all who confess Him being joined to the church to just one out of every twenty? Can those who are not really joined to the church even be called "converts" if we are going to comply with the biblical definition of that word?

How Do We Teach Disciples to Observe All?

The Apostle Paul gave a very clear outline for how disciples were to be taught to observe all that the Lord had commanded:

> **And He gave some as apostles, and some as prophets, and some as evangelists, and some as pastors and teachers,**
>
> **for the equipping of the saints for the work of service, to the building up of the body of Christ;**
>
> **until we all attain to the unity of the faith, and of the knowledge of the Son of God, to a mature man, to the measure of the stature which belongs to the fullness of Christ.**
>
> **As a result, we are no longer to be children, tossed here and there by waves, and carried about by every wind of doctrine, by the trickery of men, by craftiness in deceitful scheming;**

but speaking the truth in love, we are to
grow up in all aspects into Him who is the
head, even Christ,

from whom the whole body, being fitted
and held together by what every joint supplies,
according to the proper working of each individual part, causes the growth of the body for the
building up of itself in love (Ephesians 4:11-16).

Here we see that no one man could perform the ministry required for the church to be equipped. Jesus was the
Apostle, Prophet, Evangelist, Pastor, and Teacher. When He
ascended, He gave aspects of His ministry to many different
ones. Together these five equipping ministries formed His
complete ministry required to equip the disciples and cause
them to grow up **"in *all* aspects into Him."** It is therefore
apparent that the church will never become all that she
is called to be until all of these ministries are functioning
together as they did in the first century.

It is also obvious according to this Scripture that
if the church has not attained this stature, all of these
ministries are still needed. They were clearly given *"until*
we attain to":

1) **the unity of the faith**

2) **the knowledge of the Son of God**

3) **a mature man**

4) **the measure of the stature which belongs to the
fullness of Christ.**

Is there a church anywhere in the world that can claim this? If not, then we still need all of these ministries functioning in their places.

A main factor that seems to have constantly diverted the church and kept her from being all that she has been called to be has been the tendency to take whatever parts of the gospel we want and either reject or overlook the rest. We cannot fulfill the Great Commission until we make disciples, not just converts, and teach them to observe *all* that the Lord has commanded us.

THE POWER OF WEAKNESS

What was the gospel message preached by the first-century church? How was it presented? How does it compare to what is generally presented as the gospel today? The Apostle Paul gave the following explanation of the message he preached:

> **And when I came to you, brethren, I did not come with superiority of speech or of wisdom, proclaiming to you the testimony of God,**
>
> **For I determined to know nothing among you except Jesus Christ, and Him crucified.**
>
> **I was with you in weakness and in fear and in much trembling,**
>
> **my message and my preaching were not in persuasive words of wisdom, but in demonstration of the Spirit and power,**

> so that your faith would not rest on the wisdom of men, but on the power of God (I Corinthians 2:1-5).
>
> For the kingdom of God does not consist in words but in power (I Corinthians 4:20).

How does our preaching compare? Could it not be said that we try to come with boldness and confidence in our own persuasive words and methods more than in demonstration of the Spirit and power? Maybe this is the main reason why our results tend to be so paltry in comparison.

This is probably why the Lord sent Peter to the Jews and Paul to the Gentiles. It may seem that the Lord got these backwards, at least to our carnal way of thinking. Of course, Paul could relate to the Jews much better than Peter could, since Peter was just an ignorant fisherman. He would have been more at home with the Gentiles and they with him. The Lord called them both to the people that they would probably be the most uncomfortable with, so that they would be the most dependent on Him. Because of this, we see why Paul came to the Gentiles in **"weakness, and fear and much trembling"** (see I Corinthians 2:3).

As Paul said to the Galatians, he knew that his flesh was a trial to them (see Galatians 4:14). Both Peter and Paul were sent to preach to those who would be repelled by them in the flesh. The only way that they could fulfill their commission was to be completely dependent on the Holy Spirit. When Peter did try to go to the Gentiles, he got into trouble at Antioch (see Galatians 2:11-14). Paul insisted on going to the Jews, even though he was repeatedly warned by the Holy Spirit about what awaited him, and that insistence got him into trouble. Paul was called to go to Rome and to witness to Caesar, but there was probably an easier way for him to go there.

Christians still tend to think that we are called to the ones that have the greatest affinity or burden for. Paul unquestionably had a much greater burden for the Jews, because he declared that he would even give up his own salvation if it would lead to their salvation. Even so, Paul was not called to the Jews. Neither are we necessarily called to those for whom we may have the greatest burden to see reached. Often those desires to go to those who are the most like us are rooted in "the tyranny of the familiar" more than a genuine calling.

Paul's burden for the Jews was obviously a natural one. According to the flesh, he was the "Hebrew of Hebrews." What did Paul himself write about this very factor?

> For the mind set on the flesh is death, but the mind set on the Spirit is life and peace,

> because the mind set on the flesh is hostile toward God; for it does not subject itself to the law of God, for it is not even able to do so,

> and those who are in the flesh cannot please God (Romans 8:6-8).

> So then, brethren, we are under obligation, not to the flesh, to live according to the flesh

for if you are living according to the flesh, you must die (or could we say, "have dead works"); **but if by the Spirit you are putting to death the deeds of the body, you will live.**

For all who are being led by the Spirit of God, these are sons of God (Romans 8:12-14).

A primary factor that keeps many of us from fulfilling our callings is the tendency to try to minister to those we feel the most comfortable with, or those whom we are the most like in our flesh. This basic compromise can be an easy bridge from which we can cross to start compromising the gospel.

CHAPTER FIVE
MAKING DISCIPLES

I hope the previous chapter led you to the following important questions: When we make converts into disciples, are we making them into true disciples? Are our converts being converted by the cross or by our methodology? Are they truly being led to Jesus or to our denominations, our doctrines, or even just to us?

There has been a subtle, yet profound, perversion of the gospel in modern times. It has been changed from Jesus' coming to save us from our sins to the message that He came to save us from our troubles. This is not to imply that the Lord does not help us with our troubles, but when that is the foundation upon which someone is converted, it is a very shallow one indeed. It is this perversion that keeps many from even sharing the good news until they see someone in a certain state of desperation. We need to be in desperation to come to the Lord, not because of our problems, but because of the conviction of sin.

Only the Holy Spirit can make a true disciple. He does it by bringing the conviction of sins that casts one in desperation upon the cross to find relief. If our conversion does not start in this desperation, causing us to cling to the cross for forgiveness and as the only source of relief, we have started on the wrong foundation. There is a resurrection after the cross, but people cannot be resurrected until they have first died. To try to impart the hope and benefits of the resurrection without the death to our self-life on the cross is a terrible and tragic delusion which may have made multitudes feel better about their conditions, but could in fact still leave them in eternal jeopardy.

Jesus is not coming cap-in-hand, begging men to "accept Him." He still calls men the way He called them when He walked this earth.

> **And He was saying to them all, "If anyone wishes to come after Me, let him deny himself, and take up his cross daily, and follow Me" (Luke 9:23).**

> **"So then none of you can be My disciple who does not give up all of his own possessions" (Luke 14:33).**

> **For the love of Christ controls us, having concluded this, that one died for all, therefore all died;**

> **and He died for all, so that they who live might no longer live for themselves, but for Him who died and rose again on their behalf (II Corinthians 5:14-15).**

"Not everyone who says to Me, 'Lord, Lord,' will enter the kingdom of heaven, but he who does the will of My Father who is in heaven.

"Many will say to Me on that day, 'Lord, Lord did we not prophesy in Your name, and in Your name cast out demons, and in Your name perform many miracles?'

"And then I will declare to them, 'I never knew you; depart from Me, you who practice lawlessness'" (Matthew 7:21-23).

When Jesus called His disciples it was for total commitment—they had to be willing to leave everything to follow Him. So do we. Nothing less than this is true discipleship. When we modify the message of the cross in order to make it acceptable, we destroy the power of that message to truly save. That is why Paul said, **"For Christ did not send me to baptize, but to preach the gospel, not in cleverness of speech, so that the cross of Christ would not be made void" (I Corinthians 1:17).** Adding our own cleverness to the message of the cross in order to make it palatable to men can compromise its very power to save.

KEEPING THE FIRST COMMANDMENT FIRST

True evangelism is not founded on a love for the lost as much as on a love for the Savior. It is not a man-centered message but rather a Christ-centered one. It is when Jesus is lifted up, not our churches, not our doctrines—but Jesus, that all men will be drawn. To lift Him up, we must keep our attention upon Him. We cannot even let our love and concern for the lost eclipse our devotion to Him, or it will lead to a perversion of the gospel.

True Christianity requires being born again by God's Spirit. This rebirth *initiates* the restoring of our union with Him, but it is the beginning of this process, not its conclusion. True Christianity is a journey to intimate fellowship with our Father through Jesus Christ. It was our fellowship with the Lord that was the most tragic loss of the Fall. If there is any way that true spiritual maturity can be measured—if there is any way that we can determine the degree to which true redemption has worked in our lives, it will be by how close to Him we have become.

As we draw close to Him, becoming His disciples, we will begin to behold His glory that changes us. Let us consider what is said in II Corinthians 3:18: **"But we all, with unveiled face, beholding as in a mirror the glory of the Lord, are being transformed into the same image from glory to glory, just as from the Lord, the Spirit."**

Here we see that it is not just seeing the glory that we need, but seeing His glory *"with an unveiled face."* The veil is our flesh. When we are born again, we begin to see the kingdom of God because we are spiritually circumcised. The flesh must be cut away so that we can see Him. Even so, *we do not change so that we can fellowship with Him, but we are changed by our fellowship with Him.*

The historian Will Durant observed the following: "Caesar sought to change men by changing institutions.

Jesus changed institutions by changing men." The gospel is not about the building of an institution, but rather the building of men. When the true wine of the true gospel is preached, it will burst out of the institutions that men build like new wine will burst out of an old wineskin. The true gospel is a life too powerful to be contained in our pitiful little structures.

This does not mean that the church does not have structure and order, but it must be one that is utterly flexible if it is to contain the true wine of the Spirit. We must let the life produce the structure, not the other way around. The early church had community and met from house to house because they had life, not in order to get it. They became a force so great that when just two of them limped into their city, the powerful officials of the most powerful empire that men had ever built quaked and declared, "Those who have turned the world upside down have now come to us!" The first-century church became such a power because the church was not the pattern for their church life—Jesus was the pattern. They were not following a formula or a form but a Person.

It still seems that before the Spirit can move again in a great way, He must find those who are still "formless and void." Those who think that they have the answers, who think that they know how to build things in such a way that He will come, are almost always left behind, and the Lord has to start His new moves with those who are basically full of fear and trembling, helpless and humble, but who know and love the anointing and are willing to follow Him.

He again fixes a certain day, "Today," . . . "Today if you hear His voice, do not harden your hearts" (Hebrews 4:7).

Thus says the Lord, "Heaven is My throne and the earth is My footstool. Where then is a house you could build for Me? And where is a place that I may rest?

"For My hand made all these things, thus all these things came into being," declares the Lord. "But to this one will I look (to be His dwelling place), to him who is humble and contrite of spirit, and who trembles at My word" (Isaiah 66:1-2).

CHAPTER SIX

THE FOUNDATION OF APOSTLES

As we proceed, there will be a few purposeful redundancies. These will be for the purpose of connecting and expanding some of the most basic principles covered.

As we have covered, the life of the church in the first century was the result of one basic factor—the Lord was in their midst. They had encounters with Him day by day. He was their message, and He did works among them. The leaders of the church began their commission immediately after such great failures as denying the Lord and fleeing from Him while He was in His greatest time of need. It is probable that no one would have followed these leaders unless they were anointed. They were utterly dependent on the Lord to accomplish their purposes. Such is the nature of all who walk in true leadership. They are but earthen vessels. Our trust must not be in the vessels, but in the glory that the Lord has so mercifully allowed them to carry.

The church existed only because the Lord Himself was among them. It had no alternative plan, nothing else to fall back on. If the Lord ceased to dwell among them, then they had no reason to gather together. But the Lord was among them. He was the One doing the building, and He was the reason for their existence. It has been reported that Billy Graham once said that if the Holy Spirit left the church that most would not know anything had changed. That is a most terrible indictment, but sadly true. Therefore, our main goal as the church should be to seek the Lord's presence among us. If there are not things happening with us that absolutely cannot be credited to men, then we are in need of a most basic change.

One of the most shocking verses in the Bible has to be Revelation 3:20, where the Lord is standing at the door of His own church knocking to see if anyone will hear His voice and invite Him in! In this age, the Lord will only come where He is wanted and invited. I used to marvel at the people who would criticize John Wimber and the Vineyard Movement for inviting the Holy Spirit into their meetings, claiming that this was "not biblical." Maybe they weren't saying or doing everything just right, but the Holy Spirit was coming into the Vineyard meetings far more in those days than possibly anywhere else in the world. If you went to the meetings of these critics, you would want to pass out canteens to the people because of the dryness.

One basic thing that we can settle about the Lord's nature is that He would have far more mercy for sinners than most could understand, but He had no patience with the religious conservatives who were hypocrites. Since I am a religious conservative, I am compelled even more to understand this. Can there be religious conservatives who are also merciful and full of grace? That is a revolutionary concept, but one we need to grasp if we are to be what we are called to be. How can we maintain a sincere devotion to the biblical standards of morality, integrity, and sound doctrine, while being so full of grace and mercy that the sinners will be attracted to us like they were to Jesus?

THE APOSTOLIC MINISTRY

The first and most important thing that was lost by the fall of man was his intimate relationship to God. The whole plan of redemption that was added after the Fall was designed to restore the intimate relationship between man and God. God created man for fellowship, and His ultimate goal is to have His habitation among men. TO BE A DWELLING PLACE OF GOD IS THE ULTIMATE CALLING OF MEN. *The apostolic ministry is given to the church as a master builder for helping to build the habitation of God.*

Redemption is but the first step in restoring man's former state of fellowship with the Lord. However, the Lord's plan of redemption is much more than just restoring us to the former state before the Fall. When we are born again, we become a part of the **"new creation" (see Galatians 6:15),** which greatly transcends the original creation. Now we do not just have fellowship with God, but we are being made into His dwelling place.

God does not just fellowship with the new creation; He has come to live in us. This is much greater than what Adam, Moses, or even the disciples experienced before the

Holy Spirit was given. That is why the Lord said to the disciples that it was better for them that He go away, in the flesh, so that the Holy Spirit would come. It was truly the most glorious and awesome time for mankind—to have our Creator walking among us. Even so, it is even more awesome to have Him living *in* us!

This is not to belittle redemption, which is essential before we can even return to fellowship with God, much less become His dwelling place. Even so, we must recognize that redemption is not the goal but rather the initial step. Redemption gets us back to "ground zero," the place from which man fell, but we are called to go on from there to much greater heights. True Christianity is more than just acknowledging certain truths or even living by them. True Christianity is becoming a "new creation" that is in an even higher unity with our Creator than the first creation. God is in us! He did not come to change our thinking or just to change our behavior; He came to live in us.

The apostolic ministry is especially devoted to seeing the church become the temple of the Lord. Therefore, if there is any way to measure the overall fruitfulness of an apostolic ministry, it would be by the manifest presence of the Lord in His church. Is the church abiding in Him so that He can manifest Himself through us? We must always keep in mind that we do not change so we can fellowship with God, but we are changed *by* our fellowship with Him. That fellowship was made possible by the cross. Regardless of how mature or righteous we become, we can never enter the Lord's presence by our own merit—only with the blood.

Before the end of this age comes, there will be a movement that will restore true apostolic Christianity to the church. This can only be done by a restored apostolic ministry. The ministry that opened the church age will be the one that closes it out. The Spirit is now moving relentlessly toward that which will again be apostolic. This is our quest—to see true, apostolic Christianity restored to the earth. This is so the church can become what she is called to be—the dwelling place of His manifest presence.

What does this mean? First, it means that Jesus will be in us to do the works that He did when He walked the earth. Second, it means that the church will accurately represent Him to the world. Our words must become His words and our works His works.

As we read in the text from Ephesians 4, when all of the ministries are fully restored and functioning in the church, we will:

1) be adequately equipped for the ministry.

2) come to the unity of the faith (which is much more than just a unity around doctrine).

3) come to the full knowledge of the Son of God.

4) be raised to a mature man, the measure of the stature which belongs to Christ.

5) no longer be children (or immature).

6) no longer be tossed about by the waves, the winds of doctrine, or the trickery of men.

7) grow up in *all aspects* into the Head.

This is the apostolic commission, and it is far beyond human genius or ability. If we are going to be apostolic, our labor will not be finished until Christ is formed in His people. We must not let any other emphasis eclipse this basic work. We are looking for more than the manifestation of the sons of God—we are looking for the manifestation of the Son of God—in His people. Jesus must always be the focus of our ministries if we are to ever be truly apostolic.

As stated, the ministry of the apostle is to bear the travail of spiritual labor until Christ is formed *in* the church, not that she would come into any certain form (see Galatians 4:19). The apostles to the early church did certain things to achieve and maintain order in the congregations, but they did not emphasize any specific form, but rather the forming of Christ within.

Changing externals, such as where and how we meet, cannot in itself impart life. The early church had community and met from house to house because they had life, not in order to get life. The church is not the pattern for the church; Jesus is the pattern for the church. The church does have order and form, but when form becomes the primary emphasis, there is almost always a fall from grace.

CHAPTER SEVEN

TESTING APOSTLES

Because the church was founded by apostles who were building on the foundation of Jesus Christ, we need to define an apostle and be open to this ministry if we are going to be what we are called to be. We also live in a time when the revelation of the need for this ministry has caused many to claim being an apostle so that it is now hard to throw a rock into a crowd and not hit one who claims to one. The first century seemed to have the same problem, which is why the Lord commended the church in Ephesus: **"You put to the test those who call themselves apostles, and they are not, and you found them to be false" (see Revelation 2:2).** We will briefly try to define this ministry from the testimony of the New Testament before going on.

APOSTLES ARE SPIRITUAL FATHERS.

Paul said that we have many teachers but not many fathers (see I Corinthians 4:15). The same is true in the church today. There are many outstanding teachers and preachers, but not many fathers. Most men become fathers when they are young, so they are called fathers at a young age. Being a spiritual father has little to do with age. A spiritual father reproduces his ministry in others. Very few have done this.

Even so, just the ability to reproduce our ministry in others does not make us apostles. All of the equipping ministries are supposed to do this. To be apostolic is more than reproducing our ministry in others; it is seeing Christ formed in the whole church.

APOSTLES ESTABLISH CHURCHES

This was an obvious result of apostolic ministry in the first century. However, there is a big difference between establishing churches and building franchises. Churches in the first century were so unique that each one in the Book of Revelation needed a different word from the Lord, even though they all existed in the same general region at the same time. Our God is the blessed Creator who made every snowflake different. Possibly the single most tragic way that we have misrepresented God is by our boring uniformity. Every congregation, every person, and every meeting should be gloriously unique and interesting if we are to reflect our blessed Creator.

The Lord is the only one who can build His church. He does this through apostles, who He uses as "wise master builders." Even so, the Lord will be both the designer and builder of His own house. If we are going to be a part of a true apostolic church, we must question whether we are building something the Lord wants to dwell in or building that which will attract people. If our primary motivation is to attract people, we will not build that which will bring the manifest presence of the Lord. If we build what the Lord wants, we may or may not attract many people to it, but that is not our concern.

The Lord does care about numbers. He desires for all men to be saved and come to the knowledge of the truth. Even so, there are places where the conditions are such that His presence will not draw many people, and there are places where He will draw far more than a human organization can contain. We are not here to be big or small, but to do His will and to abide in Him so that He can abide in us.

We must also consider that just building churches does not make one an apostle. Evangelists, pastors, teachers, or prophets, as well as those who are not recognized as being one of the equipping ministries, may be used to establish churches. The first-century church at Antioch was not birthed by apostles, but it gave birth to apostles and even a new type of apostolic missionary. It is likely that if this church had been birthed by the apostolic team from Jerusalem, it may not have been able to give birth to the new type of apostle that came forth from her. Only a new wineskin can hold God's new wine. However, the Lord is also going to serve "aged, refined wine at His banquet that He is preparing for all people" (see Isaiah 25:6). We should have a taste for both!

APOSTLES IMPART GOD'S GOVERNMENT

We cannot have a revelation of who Jesus is without understanding that He is the "King of kings." Jesus is the ultimate representative of God's authority, and if we are becoming like Him, we will both walk in and help to establish His authority in the earth.

However, the Lord made it clear that His authority was not like the Gentiles or present human authority. His authority was based on love and service. The most devastating mistakes in church history have been the result of church leaders imposing church government that was in the form of present human authority rather than that of the kingdom. Present earthly authority is in contrast to the very nature and Spirit of the Lord, and it will not produce righteousness in the people.

The Lord's own leadership style is in striking contrast to that of most churches and movements throughout history, and this deserves a considerable amount of attention in our study. The Lord did not impart a system of government but built men who had government in their hearts. Even if we have the best system of government, it will be bad if we do not have good people in it. Likewise, even bad systems of government can be good with good people in them.

Presently the government of God is not a system or organization but an anointing. We only have true spiritual authority to the degree that the King lives within us. When men derive their authority from a position in a system, they can maintain influence long after the anointing has departed from them. This alone has caused repeated tragedies in church history.

However, we must also recognize that lawlessness is one of the greatest enemies at the end of the age. Though it is likely that the truth of God's government is yet to be discovered by the modern church, it will not be built upon the rebellion of tearing down what now exists. Even earthly governments that are in contrast to His nature are ordained by Him for keeping order until His kingdom comes. Let us not confuse the fact that His authority is based on love and service, but it still contains discipline and judgment.

AN APOSTLE HAS SEEN THE LORD

This is one of the criteria which Paul determined for proof of apostolic authority when defending his own ministry (see I Corinthians 9:1). This obviously means that an apostle must literally see the Lord as a prerequisite for an apostolic commission.

Jesus is the pattern of the house that the apostle is commissioned to build. Just as Moses, who built the first dwelling place of God on the earth, had to go up on the mountain and see the pattern of that dwelling place before he could build it, the apostle who is called to labor until Christ is formed must see the glory of who He now is and have this branded on his heart and mind.

When we are captured by the glory of who He is, we will not be distracted by the ways which may seem good, but are still according to man. Devotion to patterns and formulas is a basic characteristic of witchcraft, not true spiritual authority. Witchcraft is the counterfeit of true spiritual authority. If we are to be delivered from the tendency to use human devices for trying to accomplish the purposes of God, we must see Him on His throne in such a way that it is much more than a doctrine to us. It is required of true apostolic ministries that they have literally and visibly seen the resurrected Christ.

THE APOSTLE IS A WITNESS OF HIS RESURRECTION

This is related to the last point, which is to have seen Him in His resurrection glory, but it also speaks of proclaiming His resurrection. It is by seeing the glory of His resurrection that our proclamation is empowered.

In Acts 1:22, we see that the office of the apostle was given to be a witness of His resurrection. In Acts 4:33, we see that power was given to the church to be a witness of His resurrection. In Romans 1:4, we see that Jesus **"was declared the Son of God with power by the resurrection from the dead."**

The resurrection was the central theme of the gospel that was preached by the first-century apostles. Yet having studied the writings and messages of the great voices from church history, it is hard to find more than a cursory address of this most foundational truth by any of them. I have listened to thousands of sermons—many by some of the greatest preachers of our own time, and I do not recall a single in-depth message being given on this subject unless it was an obligatory Easter sermon. Could the neglect of this most basic truth be a primary reason why the church today is so far from the apostolic pattern and power of the first-century church? I think so.

Charles Spurgeon went so far as to say, "There are very few *Christians* who believe in the resurrection." When I first read this I thought that it was a misprint, but then the Holy Spirit witnessed to me that it was true. True faith is more than just an intellectual assent to certain facts. It is by believing in our *hearts,* not our minds, which results in righteousness (see Romans 10:10). We can believe in the doctrine of the resurrection without truly believing it in our hearts. If we truly believed in our hearts, most of our lives would be radically different than they are now. We would not be as consumed with the tyranny of the temporary and would be given fully to the things that are eternal. What Spurgeon was implying is that we give intellectual assent to the fact of the resurrection but go on living our lives as if it did not exist. Paul wrote in I Corinthians 15:13-14, if we do not believe in the resurrection, our faith is in vain.

Apostolic Vision

Moses was a man of vision. He actually saw the Tabernacle in detail on the Mount before he began its construction (see Exodus 25:40). A true spiritual vision is not just something that we decide to come up with—*a true spiritual vision must originate with God.*

The Prophet Haggai said that **"the latter glory of this house will be greater than the former" (see Haggai 2:9).** He did not say that the latter house would be greater but that the glory in it would be greater. The apostolic goal is not focused on the house as much as on the glory of the

One who is to inhabit the house. True apostolic vision is Christ-centered, not church-centered. The apostolic call is to lead men to Christ, not just to church.

If men are truly led to Christ, they will end up in church, but the reverse is not necessarily true. Many are drawn to the church for various reasons but never come to know the Lord. What good is the most glorious temple if the Lord is not in it? If He is in it, the temple will not be what gets our attention. The great apostolic prayer was the following:

> I pray that the eyes of your heart may be enlightened, so that you will know what is the hope of *His* calling, what are the riches of the glory of *His* inheritance in the saints,
>
> and what is the surpassing greatness of *His* power toward us who believe. These are in accordance with the working of the strength of *His* might (Ephesians 1:18-19).

It does not say that we should come to know what is the hope of *our* calling or *our* inheritance. Neither will anything of true eternal value ever be accomplished by *our* power. One of the most subtle but devastating deceptions that we can fall into is the over-emphasis of who we are in Christ in place of who He is in us. We need to know who we are and what our callings are, but we must never allow this to eclipse our devotion to seeing Him.

APOSTOLIC GIFTING

Because apostles are called to be God's master builders for His dwelling place, the church, we can see aspects of the character required for this task in the lives of all who were used to build His dwelling places in Scripture. Of Moses, the first to build a dwelling place for God, this was said:

> **By faith Moses, when he was come to years, refused to be called the son of Pharaoh's daughter;**
>
> **choosing rather to suffer affliction with the people of God, than to enjoy the pleasures of sin for a season;**
>
> **esteeming the reproach of Christ greater riches than the treasures in Egypt; for he had respect unto the** (spiritual) **recompense of the reward (Hebrews 11:24-26 KJV).**

Here we see that he chose to sacrifice the greatest of worldly opportunities to serve the purpose of God, refusing to be called the son of Pharaoh's daughter. The Apostle Paul, as the archetype of the biblical apostle, did the same, refusing the high position of influence he could have attained as the Pharisee of Pharisees.

Moses chose to suffer affliction with the people of God, esteeming the sufferings of Christ as **"greater riches"** than all of the treasures of Egypt. Paul also walked in continual persecution, dangers, and setbacks, viewing all of them as making greater opportunities for the gospel and even a basis for his authority.

As a Roman citizen, Paul was obviously in a high position as a member of the aristocracy of the world's greatest empire, yet by his own admission he counted every such title and privilege "as dung" (see Philippians 3:7). Just as the earth does not register as much more than a speck of dust in the great expanse of God's universe, all of the riches of this earth could not be compared to a speck of dust in the eternal dwelling place of God. To suffer any kind of persecution for the sake of His gospel is a treasure far beyond any earthly wealth.

Moses rejected the temporary pleasures of sin. All of the apostles walked in a life above reproach, sanctified and holy to the Lord. They were examples to the church, but they did not do this just to be examples. They dwelt in the presence of a holy God. When we view the beauty of His holiness, we will hate even the garment tainted by sin. God is holy, and we cannot truly love Him without loving purity. Just as Moses *chose* to suffer affliction for the purposes of God, we too have a choice as to whether we sin or not. If we are to be an apostolic church, we must begin to choose to walk uprightly before the Lord.

Moses' vision was on the (spiritual) recompense of the reward. It is often said that some people are so heavenly-minded that they are not any earthly good. Those about whom this is said may be close to being apostolic. What men who ever walked the earth after Jesus were more heavenly-minded than the apostles? An overwhelming problem in the ministry today is that most are too earthly-minded to be any spiritual good.

"For he (Moses) **endured as** *seeing him who is invisible"* **(see Hebrews 11:27 KJV).** Spiritual vision requires that what we see with the eyes of our hearts will be more real to us than what we see with our natural eyes. *We must see that which is invisible to others.*

Scriptures such as Ephesians 4 make it clear that the apostolic ministry must be restored to the church before the end comes. The apostolic message cannot be in word only, but in demonstration of the Spirit and power. One can comply with all of the things listed previously and yet still not be an apostle. The apostolic ministry requires a commission from God, and it requires the substance of spiritual authority. True apostles will not be coming just with theories, forms, recipes, and formulas but with an impartation of the life of Christ which will produce true church life. That is nothing less than to be the temple of God—to dwell in His presence and to manifest the sweet aroma of the knowledge of Him in every place. Before the end, such a church will turn the world upside down again.

As stated, the Lord praised the church at Ephesus because they **"put to the test those who call themselves apostles, and they are not" (see Revelation 2:2).** We cannot allow our spiritual currency to be devalued by calling those apostles who do not qualify. Even so, just as we must receive a prophet "in the name of a prophet" to receive a prophet's reward, the same is true of every ministry. If we receive an apostle as just a teacher, we will not get the full reward of having received an apostle—all we will get is teaching. It is right that we put to the test those who call themselves apostles and reject those who are not, but let us also be looking expectantly for those who really are and receive them properly in order to receive the full reward of their ministry.

For those who would like to study the apostolic ministry further, I have covered it in much more depth in my book, *The Apostolic Ministry,* which is available in many Christian bookstores, from MorningStar Ministries at www.MorningStarMinistries.org, or by calling 1-800-542-0278.

CHAPTER EIGHT

THE FOUNDATION OF PROPHETS

Prophets were also very much a part of the life of the early church. However, if we take the New Testament as a measure of how common they were, there were not as many prophets as there were apostles. That is not necessarily accurate, but we can say that prophets were not mentioned as much as the apostles. This is understandable because apostles were doing the main work of establishing the church, and it appears that all of the apostles were also prophets. Even so, the prophets are highlighted in the New Testament, and, at times, their ministries are spectacular.

In the narrative of the New Testament and the other writings of the time, it seems the fact that there were prophets was taken for granted by believers even though their influence was significant and widespread. Paul wrote in Ephesians 2:19-22:

> **So then you are no longer strangers and aliens, but you are fellow citizens with the saints, and are of God's household,**

having been built upon the foundation of the apostles and prophets, Christ Jesus Himself being the corner stone,

in whom the whole building, being fitted together, is growing into a holy temple in the Lord,

in whom you also are being built together into a dwelling of God in the Spirit.

A primary purpose of the prophetic ministry was to speak to the church on God's behalf. Although every ministry in a sense speaks for the Lord, the prophetic words given by prophets tended to speak of major future events or to a specific situation with a specific revelation of the will and purpose of God concerning it.

NEW COVENANT PROPHETIC MINISTRY

There is also a difference between Old Covenant prophets and New Covenant prophets. Under the Old Covenant, the prophets often stood alone or in small groups of prophets and spoke to the nation or nations. With the birth of the church, the prophet was but one member of a team of ministries given to equip the church. Because of this, the most prevalent place of prophets in the New Testament was working with the apostles.

Under the Old Covenant, prophets had a major position of influence and actually wrote most of the Old Testament. New Testament prophets are often compared to them and expected to be like them, but this was obviously not the case in the early church. Under the Old Covenant, prophets were the primary source of correction and warning about the judgments of God. In the New Testament, we do not have a single example of a prophet being used this way in the church. The prophet Agabus gave a prophecy about a famine that was to come upon the whole world, but it was not described as judgment, and he did not bring a corrective word with it. In reading the works of the early church fathers, I do not recall a single example of prophets bringing such correction to the church either. This seems to have become the work of the apostles rather than the prophets, and I would expect the prophets were very happy about this!

The prophets in the early church seemed to have functioned somewhat like the nervous system in the body, which carries signals from the brain to the rest of the body. Although its primary function is to represent the head and connect it to the rest of the body, the nervous system also carries some signals (such as pain) from the body back to the brain. The prophet, likewise, stood in the place of both messenger and intercessor.

The Lord has by no means limited Himself to speaking only through those called as prophets, but that is the primary function of a prophet. Similarly, even though the Lord may choose to use anyone for healing the sick, whether the person has a special gift of healing or not, the one who has this gift will be especially devoted to it. The Apostle Paul explained that everyone is not a foot or an eye. **"If the whole body were an eye, where would the hearing be?"** (see I Corinthians 12:17).

Paul also said, **"You can all prophesy one by one"** (see **I Corinthians 14:31**). Even though the foot is not the eye, when it is dark and one cannot use his eyes, he may stick out his foot to "see" where he is going. While the Lord does appoint many believers to specialize in a ministry, it does not mean those are the only ones He will ever use for that ministry. Not everyone is a prophet, but all may prophesy.

Every member of the body is different. We cannot expect other ministers to be like prophets, nor the prophets to be like other ministers. Actually, every prophet in Scripture was different from all of the other prophets. It is a fundamental nature of the Lord to be creative. He makes every person, every tree, and even every snowflake different. When we limit the Lord, or the things of the Lord, to a certain pattern or formula, we have greatly limited our ability to relate to Him and hear from Him.

Even though the function of the New Covenant prophets seems to have differed greatly from their Old Covenant counterparts, their prophetic gifts and the ways that they received revelation from God seem to have been the same. Some prophets under both covenants received revelation through visions, dreams, by the word of the Lord, by discerning His purposes in current events, through the Scriptures, and some by trances, which is kind of like falling into a dream when you are awake. Some were caught up into the spiritual realm so that they were not just seeing a vision—they were there. Others received revelation from angels and others directly from the Lord. He may speak to us one way now and the next time speak to us in an entirely different manner. He does not do this to confuse us but to keep us seeking and dependent on Him.

PROPHETS OF CHRIST

"The testimony of Jesus is the spirit of prophecy" (see Revelation 19:10). All true prophecy is His testimony. It comes from Him and is intended to draw us to Him. It is what He is saying to His church. Jesus has manifested Himself in different ways—He is a lion, and He is also a lamb. He came as the Prince of Peace, and yet He said He came to bring a sword. These aspects of His nature do not contradict; they complement each other and give us a more complete revelation of Him.

This is why the apostle entreated the Romans to **"behold then the kindness and severity of God" (see Romans 11:22).** We must behold both His kindness and His severity if we are to have an accurate revelation of His nature. Those who only see His kindness, mercy, and forgiveness have almost inevitably fallen into the error of presumptuous grace and unsanctified mercy. Unsanctified mercy is having mercy for things of which God disapproves. Those who only see His severity often become "sheep beaters" who minister more in the spirit of **"the accuser of our brethren" (see Revelation 12:10)** than in the Spirit of Jesus, who lives to intercede for us (see Hebrews 7:25).

New Testament prophets were not "prophets of grace" or "prophets of judgment," but rather prophets who gave the testimony of Jesus. That testimony can be different for different countries and even different parts of countries, or different churches. Those who preach or prophesy must be sensitive to what Jesus is saying in the place where they are and must not just come with a general message of kindness or severity. If we carry the general message of severity to those who are already beaten down by the accuser, we will be feeding that condemning spirit instead of the Spirit and testimony of Jesus. The same is true if we are prone to only preach His kindness. The true prophet will not be "locked in" to a message of mercy, judgment, or any other position, but will speak the present mind of Christ for each situation.

When John received the Revelation, each of the seven churches in Asia Minor needed a different message, even though they existed in the same region at the same period of time. This shows that when we try to give a single message to the whole church, we will seldom truly have the mind of the Lord. John received these messages for the churches by being caught up in the Spirit and receiving them from the Lord, not by going to the churches and trying to judge their conditions or needs. Pastors and teachers can sometimes discern the needs for shepherding and teaching by just being with a church and observing it, but that is not how prophets operate. To give the appropriate prophetic message to a church, we must see the Lord, not the people.

Jesus is the Lion and the Lamb. Sometimes He speaks in a **"still small voice" (see I Kings 19:12 KJV)**, and at other times He **"roars from Zion"** (see Joel 3:16). If we can only hear the still small voice, we will miss Him when He roars and vice versa. It is not how God speaks that enables us to recognize Him—it is the Spirit that is speaking that we must discern. I know my wife's voice whether she whispers or raises her voice because I know her. If we know the Lord, we will recognize His voice regardless of the manner in which He speaks.

THE EQUIPPING PURPOSE OF PROPHETIC MINISTRY

The Lord's ultimate goal through the New Testament prophetic ministry is not just to give the church prophecies, but to bring the church to the place where we **"can all prophesy"** (see I Corinthians 14:31). The prophets, like the other equipping gift ministries, are not given just to perform their own ministry, but for **"the equipping of the saints for the work of service"** (see Ephesians 4:12).

The New Testament prophet's primary function is to open the church to the ministry of Jesus the Prophet so that He can flow freely among His people. Not everyone is called to the office of a prophet, but the whole church, as a unit, is called to be a prophet to the world, manifesting Christ's ministry as the Spokesman for God.

When Israel was told to partake of the Passover, they were told that they had to eat the entire lamb and **"not leave any of it"** (see Exodus 12:10). We must receive all of Jesus if we are to receive Him at all. Paul instructed the Corinthians, **"The testimony concerning Christ was confirmed in you, so that you are not lacking in any** gift" (I Corinthians 1:7). The true testimony of Christ is confirmed in the church when He is able to freely move in any way that He chooses. This is profound evidence that He has found a place to lay His head—a place where He is the Head.

We must understand that ministries seldom come in the packages that we would expect. The Lord chooses the foolish things of the world to confound the wise (see I Corinthians 1:27). As stated, He chose Paul, the Pharisee of Pharisees, to be the apostle of grace. He chose Peter, the most unstable of the twelve, to be *Petra*, the rock. If we allow His grace to work, He will make some of the most unlikely people into mighty apostles and prophets. Likewise, some of the vessels who appear most promising in our eyes will prove to be false.

THE "DRY BONES" TEST

It seems that every one called to be a prophet must pass the test of Ezekiel 37. What do we see in the present valley of dry bones? Those without vision will only see death. As this lesson in Ezekiel 37 was intended to teach Ezekiel, the prophet must learn to see in even the driest bones an exceedingly great army and begin to prophesy life to those bones until they become what they are called to be. This is one of the ultimate purposes of the prophetic ministry given to the church—to call the church forth to her destiny.

Coming into true unity will not happen just by getting together, but only as we are all beholding the One who holds all things together **"by the word of His power" (see Hebrews 1:3)**. Anyone can see Babylon, but who can see the majesty of the city God is building? That requires prophetic vision—seeing beyond the way things are to the One in whom everything in heaven and earth will be summed up.

There is much more that can and needs to be addressed about this foundation laying ministry given to the church, and we will address it in time. For now, we can conclude by the Scriptures that it is a crucial ministry given to the church along with apostles for laying the foundation. The foundation will not be properly laid without them. It was true in the first century, and it will be true to the end of this age, when finally we will no longer need prophets because all will know His voice.

For those who would like to study the prophetic ministry further, I have covered it in more depth in my book, *The Prophetic Ministry*. I would also like to recommend Steve Thompson's book titled, *You May All Prophesy*, which has been called the most clear and practical study of this ministry by theologians and Christian leaders alike. These are both available in many Christian bookstores, from MorningStar Ministries at www.MorningStarMinistries.org, or by calling 1-800-542-0278.

CHAPTER NINE
THE LIFE OF THE EARLY CHURCH

The life of the church in the first century was the result of one basic factor—the Lord was in their midst. They had encounters with Him daily. He was their message, and He did works among them. He did the works through the apostles, but also through any believer He chose to move through at any time. Church was twenty-four hours a day, seven days a week. They did not go to church—they were the church.

In the beginning, the apostles taught in the temple daily, but then the people met from house to house. When God is not moving, meetings can be a burden, but when He is moving, all the people of God want to do is meet. When God is moving in His people, there simply is no greater home for the soul—nothing more wonderful, exciting, or fulfilling than experiencing Him together with His people in authentic church life.

God made man to need Him and to need one another. This is why loneliness is the first thing that the Lord said was not good about His creation: **"It is not good for man to be alone" (see Genesis 2:18).** God said this when man was with Him! Adam had God and the animals, but those were not enough for him. This is because God made Adam that way. Adam needed God, but he also needed fellowship with his own kind. We need God more than other people, but we need other people too. God made us all that way.

Of course, there should be times when we need to get alone to seek the Lord, and our personal relationship with Him should be deeper and more wonderful than our relationships with even the closest people in our lives, but this does not mean we do not need other people too. As Bonhoeffer observed in his classic work on Christian community, those who need community more than they need God need to learn to be alone with the Lord, and those who only want to be alone with the Lord need community. The most healthy, balanced Christian life will have both.

The two greatest commandments are to love God and to love one another. Loving God must always be first. If we do not love God above others, we will not love others the way we should. However, we are also told that we cannot love God without also loving one another (see I John 4:20). True love for God will always find an expression for loving His people as well. These two commandments are also one—they go together.

It is hard to read the account of the first-century church and not long for what they had. One of the most descriptive words used to describe the church in the New Testament was *fellowship*. The English word *fellowship* is derived from the phrase "two fellows in a ship," implying that for them to go anywhere, they would have to work together. That is a good metaphor, but the Greek word used for fellowship was *koinonia,* which indicated a deeper interweaving of one another. Another English word used when translating *koinonia* is *communion,* or *common-union.* The fellowship of the saints in the New Testament was such a deep, interconnecting weaving of their lives together that their identity with the "holy nation" of the church was greater than any other national or cultural identity—this was the true sense of what family was intended to be.

All Christians were called "saints," which means "true believers." Because of the danger of being a Christian, it was quite certain that all who were in the fellowship were true believers. No doubt this fellowship was wonderful, but it was also hard. It took anointed and wise leadership to resolve disputes. There was persecution and even martyrdom. Not only were they under constant threat from without because of the authorities, but there were also heresies that arose from within that divided the young churches. Some fell into grievous sins—all of which had to be terribly discouraging at times. For the believers to have held together through all that was assaulting them, there must have been a very powerful fellowship with the Lord and with one another.

Many esteem the first-century church, and even the very first church in Jerusalem, as the perfect model of what church life is called to be. It is still probable that they may have been the greatest church yet in history. However, there is evidence that the apostles themselves did not think that the church in those early stages was the ultimate of what church life was supposed to be, but instead just the beginning of something that would mature into an even more wonderful and powerful temple of the Lord made out of living stones. They looked at what was recorded in the Book of Acts as a seed, not the fruit. Even so, the fruit may be much more than the seed, but the seed carries within it the DNA of what the fruit will be. For this reason, there is great merit in studying the seed of what the church is called to be, but we do need to keep in mind that we are not trying to be another first-century church, but rather the twenty-first century church.

The first-century church had so many enemies that it seemed the whole world was trying to snuff them out. Yet the church not only survived, but grew and ultimately changed the world more than any other religion, philosophy, or conqueror had ever done. From the outside, the church must have appeared to be the most frail of all societies, yet there has never been anything as powerful in human history. Even today, if the church functions on even a tiny fraction of her potential, she will be by far the most powerful force on the planet.

When the church comes into the unity that has been prophesied, it will truly be an irresistible force and an immovable object. Because of this there is no one who can lead it except the Lord Jesus Himself. It can only come into unity as it "holds fast to the Head" (see Colossians 2:19). The power of the first-century church was Jesus manifested in their midst. This alone can also bring us into our intended destiny. Even so, He manifested Himself through His people—all of them.

At first, the teaching and the great works were done through the apostles, but after about eight years, the Lord was manifesting Himself with the same kind of power through many of the common believers. Stephen, the first Christian martyr, who was also one of the first to be appointed a deacon to serve tables, arose in such power in word and miracles that it seemed his works eclipsed even the apostles as he became the primary focus of the persecution.

Later, after the Apostle Paul was converted on the road to Damascus, the Lord gave a common believer, Ananias, a vision to instruct him to go to a specific address and then told him what to say to Paul (at that time called "Saul"). He then laid hands on Paul, who was immediately healed of blindness. This kind of specific direction and power being released through common believers seemed to have been quite normal at the time. This was evidence that the apostles had done their work, equipping the saints to do the work of the ministry. The church was becoming a functioning body where all of the members were working.

It is also apparent that angelic visitations were quite common, even to the point where Paul wrote that they entertained angels at times and were not aware of it (see Hebrews 13:2). When Peter was imprisoned and was about to be executed, an angel was sent to release him. When Peter appeared at the gate of the house where they were praying for him, they assumed that it was Peter's angel instead, obviously having more faith that an angel would be at the door than Peter.

Few things stir zeal for the Lord and His work like the expectation of being used by Him at any time. First-century church life was certainly not the spectator sport that much of modern Christianity has become—it was a radical life of the most exciting adventure ever known. At any time, anyone could be used to do great exploits in the name of the Lord because believers did not just sit under the apostles' teaching, they emulated their work.

When the great persecution came upon the church in Jerusalem so that the church was scattered abroad, the believers were preaching the gospel wherever they went, and churches began to spring up all across the land. In Antioch, the saints preached to the Gentiles, who embraced the word and were converted. This became one of the most important churches in the first century, and it was not even planted by apostles, yet it was used to give birth to an extraordinary new kind of apostle—the missionary apostle.

Apostolic Character

Even though the ministry of the apostles produced believers who would then go and do the same things, the apostles were the leadership of the first-century church, giving it definition and direction. For this reason, we will look at this ministry in a bit more depth.

As we have covered, the apostles began their commission immediately after such failures as denying the Lord and fleeing from Him while He was in His greatest time of need. The people knew this about their leaders and would have had a difficult time following them if it had not been for the anointing that they carried. The Holy Spirit had transformed them. No longer were they the meek cowards who had fled from opposition and persecution. They were such bold witnesses that the most powerful men in the world would stand in awe and fear of them. Such seemed to be the nature of all true apostles—everywhere they went there was definite commotion. They walked in a spiritual authority that caused great spiritual agitation.

Without the Holy Spirit, we can accomplish nothing. With Him, we can accomplish anything—including confronting the greatest darkness of our times and driving it back. With the Holy Spirit, there is no opposition that cannot be withstood, and no task that is given to us that cannot be accomplished. Because of the profound change that had come upon the believers when the Holy Spirit descended, they knew without question the Source of their power, and it turned them into bold, fearless witnesses like the prophets of old. They preached like the prophets in the Old Testament; they could stand and testify without fear before kings and potentates, and they performed great miracles. They also did something the prophets had never done—they built the temple of the Lord out of living stones—His people.

As you read the New Testament, the writings of the early church fathers and the classic writings of those who had an impact throughout the church age, there is something sown throughout their message that is rarely heard in the Western church today—the cross—a life of sacrifice. This, too, was a source of their power. They did not love their own lives, but they daily sacrificed their own desires to do His will. This brought forth a character that had not been found in a community before, and it was a force that no amount of opposition could defeat.

The true apostolic ministry still requires suffering. True Christianity is a life of sacrifice. It requires that in everything we live for the Lord and others, not ourselves. Paul wrote to the Corinthians:

> **But we have this treasure in earthen vessels, so that the surpassing greatness of the power may be of God and not from ourselves;**
>
> **we are afflicted in every way, but not crushed; perplexed, but not despairing;**
>
> **persecuted, but not forsaken; struck down, but not destroyed;**
>
> *always carrying about in the body the dying of Jesus, so that the life of* **Jesus also may be manifested in our body.**
>
> **For we who live are constantly being delivered over to death for Jesus' sake, so that the life of Jesus also may be manifested in our mortal flesh (II Corinthians 4:7-11).**

The apostles had the power to impart spiritual life to the degree that the dying of Jesus worked in them, laying aside their own lives for His sake. Death is the path to life in Christ. If we will have the true faith, there is no other path, as the Lord Himself made clear:

> Then Jesus said to His disciples, "If anyone desires to come after Me, let him *deny himself*, and take up his cross, and follow Me.
>
> "For whoever desires to save his life shall lose it, but whoever loses his life for My sake will find it" (Matthew 16:24-25 NKJV).

To deny ourselves is almost unheard of in the world, then or now. It is a foreign mentality to fallen human beings, but to the true followers of Christ, it is their nature. If it becomes the nature of the church again, the church will again prevail against the gates of hell. We are exhorted in Philipians 1:28-29:

> in no way alarmed by your opponents— which is a sign of destruction for them, but of salvation for you, and that too, from God.
>
> For to you it has been granted for Christ's sake, not only to believe in Him, but also to suffer for His sake.

This was addressed to all believers, not just apostles. The principles of sacrifice that we see attributed to biblical apostles were the same for all believers. However, the apostles, as leaders, had to be first to lay down their lives as living sacrifices. With but a few exceptions, they finished their course in martyrdom. Paul wrote to the Romans:

> The Spirit Himself bears witness with our spirit that we are children of God,

> and if children, then heirs—heirs of God
> and joint heirs with Christ, if indeed we suffer
> with Him, that we may also be glorified together
> (Romans 8:16-17 NKJV).

"If" is one of the biggest words in Scripture. It implies an absolute condition. We are told that we are heirs of God and fellow heirs with Christ "if" we suffer with Him. That is why Paul also wrote the following:

> that I may know Him and the power of His
> resurrection and the fellowship of His sufferings,
> being conformed to His death;
>
> *in order that* I may attain to the resurrection
> from the dead.
>
> Not that I have already obtained it, or have
> already become perfect, *but I* press on so that I
> may lay hold of that for which also I was laid hold
> of by *Christ Jesus* (Philippians 3:10-12).

Amazingly, Paul wrote this near the end of his life. Having endured and accomplished so much, he was still pressing on, not feeling as though he had yet accomplished his full purpose. How often do we start feeling content after just a few accomplishments and begin to rest more on what we have done than on pressing ahead until we have fully completed our course in victory? There was no thought of retirement with the apostles! Peter said this:

> Therefore, since Christ has suffered in the
> flesh, arm yourselves also with the same purpose,
> because he who has suffered in the flesh has
> ceased from sin,

> so as to live the rest of the time in the flesh
> no longer for the lusts of men, but for the will of
> God (I Peter 4:1-2).

Our time in this life is not for our happiness but for the will of God. Even so, there is no greater joy or peace that we can know in this life than that which comes from doing the will of God. If our own satisfaction is our purpose, we will not find it there, and we will also sacrifice the greatest of satisfactions for eternity, just as Paul wrote in I Corinthians 9:24-27:

> Do you not know that those who run a race
> all run, but only one receives the prize? Run in
> such a way that you may win.

> Everyone who competes in the games exer-
> cises self-control in all things. They then do
> it to receive a perishable wreath, but we an
> imperishable.

> Therefore I run in such a way, as not without
> aim; I box in such a way, as not beating the air;

> but I discipline my body and make it my
> slave, so that, after I have preached to others, I
> myself should be disqualified.

We see here the principle that to the degree we live by the law of sacrifice, we will receive and be able to give spiritual life.

Those who look at the life of sacrifice and think about how dreary it must be have never tasted of the true glory and power of the cross. There is no greater freedom that a soul can experience than to be Christ's slave. There is no greater life and joy that one can experience than having been crucified with Him and to be truly dead to this world. What can threaten a dead man? A dead man has no fears of failure, rejection, or any other fear. A crucified life does not envy or worry but will rather know the ultimate peace, patience, and love for others—the greatest joy a soul can experience in this life. The cross is the path to true life, a resurrected life, which cannot be destroyed. That is true church life.

As the apostles gave abundant demonstration of the life of the cross, courage, and boldness to proclaim Christ and the whole message of life, the church likewise took on this character. Forced human sacrifice was common in most nations some time in their history, but this was a whole new and unprecedented thing to see people willingly sacrificing their lives for a belief. This had a powerful impact wherever the gospel was preached.

THE COMMUNITY

Other aspects of life in the first-century church will be covered later. One of the most interesting of these is how the Jerusalem church actually sold all of their property and had all things in common. Nothing like this seemed to have happened before anywhere in the world, and it seems to have worked quite well in Jerusalem. However, because even those who had been a part of this never seemed to recommend it as a course of action for any other church, many have concluded that it actually did not work out that well.

There could be another answer to why this type of lifestyle was not promoted again in the first century—that it was an important precept of the Jerusalem church because of the impending catastrophe in the destruction of Jerusalem in 70 A.D. It was reported that all of the Christians escaped this destruction. Having no property or belongings to hold them back, they were free to leave as the disaster approached.

For whatever reason, this was never duplicated in the early church. It was a remarkable thing for all of the new believers to give up their own belongings for the common good, and this is certainly worth studying in more depth, which we will do. Because of the biblical prophecies of the times of trouble at the end of the church age, it could be that at times, and in certain places, the church will need to do this again.

Other aspects of life in the church community, such as the system of justice that was implemented, are worthy of more in-depth study, which we will also do later, but for now we want to focus on some more of the spiritual foundations of church life in the first century.

CHAPTER TEN
WAR OF THE SOUL

Certainly the early church life was one of the most exciting and fulfilling one could experience—as well as one of the most difficult. It was obviously intended to be this way. The Lord Jesus had the right to bind Satan and cast him into the lake of fire immediately after His resurrection. He left the devil on the loose for our sakes. He, "the last Adam," was looking for a bride that would resist the serpent, not succumb to its wiles. She was called to rule and reign with Him, not only over the earth, but also to judge the angels. She had to prove herself worthy.

Besides the constant attacks and persecutions from the civil governments and authorities, first-century Christians fought the same battles we do against the old, carnal nature. In fact, the New Testament Epistles make it very clear that this was a far bigger battle for believers than the persecutions and outward attacks. Therefore, before proceeding, we need to examine how they confronted what was arising from this carnal nature because we too must fight that battle. There is also prophetic inspiration from the Scriptures that the battle will be won by His people at the end of this age, when His bride will be the glorious beauty He deserves, **"without a spot or wrinkle" (see Ephesians 5:27 NLT).**

One of the great exhortations on this battle against **"the flesh"** is in Romans 8:6, 13-19:

> **For the mind set on the flesh is death, but the mind set on the Spirit is life and peace.**

> **for if you are living according to the flesh, you must die; but if by the Spirit you are putting to death the deeds of the body, you will live.**

> **For all who are being led by the Spirit of God, these are sons of God.**

> **For you have not received a spirit of slavery leading to fear again, but you have received a spirit of adoption as sons by which we cry out, "Abba! Father!"**

> **The Spirit Himself testifies with our spirit that we are children of God,**

> **and if children, heirs also, heirs of God and fellow heirs with Christ, *IF* indeed we suffer with Him so that we may also be glorified with Him.**

> **For I consider that the sufferings of this present time are not worthy to be compared with the glory that is to be revealed to us.**

> **For the anxious longing of the creation waits eagerly for the revealing of the sons of God.**

Adam lived in a perfect world and yet chose to sin. The whole creation that was under his authority suffered because of his transgression. Since then the whole creation has been waiting for those who will live in the darkest of times and yet choose to obey, laying down their own lives for the sake of those under their authority.

The kingdom of God is the domain of God. It is the return of His dominion to the earth for which we are serving the Lord. The first Adam fell and gave his domain over to the evil one who he had obeyed. As the "last Adam," Jesus remained faithful in order to return the domain of Adam to the Father. We become joint heirs with Him over this domain as we prove our faithfulness by living for Him and not ourselves. This sacrifice is incomprehensible to the fallen human nature, but it is the path to true life and a life that will last forever.

Paul exhorted, **"Through many tribulations we must enter the kingdom of God" (see Acts 14:22)**. This is a basic spiritual principle—that we enter the kingdom through tribulations. We all want to claim "kingdom living," but are we willing to go through the gate? This principle applies to us as individuals as well as to the whole creation. The kingdom age is going to be issued in through a great tribulation. We must therefore view tribulations as blessings and not as curses. They are gates for entering into the full purpose of God.

> **Consider it all joy, my brethren, when you encounter various trials, knowing that the testing of your faith produces endurance.**

And let endurance have its perfect result, so that you may be perfect and complete, lacking in nothing (James 1:2-4).

One of the most important lessons for all believers to learn is not to waste their trials. Every one of them is an opportunity to enter the kingdom. Peter stated:

In this you greatly rejoice, even though now for a little while, *if necessary,* you have been distressed by various trials,

so that the proof of your faith, being more precious than gold which is perishable, even though tested by fire, may be found to result in praise and glory and honor at the revelation of Jesus Christ (I Peter 1:6-7).

If we just esteemed the dealings of God even half as much as we tend to esteem earthly riches, the church would again be turning the world upside down with the power of the gospel. When we learn to esteem them according to their true value, we will again impact the whole world with the gospel. For this reason the Psalmist wrote this: **"Precious in the sight of the Lord is the death of His godly ones" (Psalm 116:15).** The Lord esteems the death of His people because He knows that it is only when we are willing to lay down our lives that we will truly find them.

Before there can be a resurrection, there must be a death. Before we can walk in resurrection power, we must first die to our own self-lives. This is probably the single aspect of Christianity that has been the most avoided since the first century. It is certainly the main reason why the world has witnessed so little of true, apostolic Christianity since. We have allowed glib clichés, such as, "They are so heavenly-minded that they are not any earthly good," to rob us of sound, biblical truth that reveals the true nature of our calling. The truth is that we have been so earthly-minded that we have had very little true spiritual power. Before the end of this age, this will change. True, apostolic Christianity will be revealed on the earth again. When it has been recovered, the kingdom will come, and the whole creation will end its long travail for the return of her Creator.

The Fall began when Satan began looking at his own, God-imparted glory. When pride entered, he turned to his own way and carried with him all who were prone to live for themselves rather than for their Creator. Jesus, who had much greater glory being the very Son of God, through even the greatest of trials did not think of Himself but only of the Father's interests. Those who will be heirs with Him will be trusted with greater glory than Satan ever knew, as they too will be His sons and daughters. They will have proven that they love truth and they love the Lord more than they love their own lives.

Those who have been emptied of self-will and selfish ambition will be filled with His glory. Such will be the ones who are worthy to be the bride of the Lamb. This lifestyle, which is so foreign to the self-preservation of the fallen world, puts the ax to the very root of the tree that has released all of the present evil into the world. It is therefore the most threatening and incomprehensible challenge to the present spirit of the world and therefore, the greatest witness of the kingdom of God.

Again, the foundation of the church is Jesus Christ. This is more than just the teaching about Him, as we see in the first-century church; it is the Lord Himself moving in their midst. The history of the early church is essentially the recorded deeds of God moving among them. The church was not built on creeds or programs, but on a living relationship with Jesus Christ, who demonstrated His presence with them day by day. The church was not recognized just by the doctrines that it held to, but by the Presence of the Lord in their midst. Such was the nature of the true church in the beginning, and such will be the nature of the true church at the end. As Peter and John stood before the Sanhedrin, we see a good example of this:

> **Now as they observed the confidence of Peter and John and understood that they were uneducated and untrained men, they were amazed, *and* began to recognize them as having been with Jesus.**
>
> **And seeing the man who had been healed standing with them, they had nothing to say in reply (Acts 4:13-14).**

Those who "had been with Jesus" were easily recognized. It is to the degree that we abide in Him, spend time with Him, and walk with Him that we will again be recognized as being true believers. When this happens, like the early apostles, we, too, will have the evidence that He is in our midst by those who stand with us because they will be healed.

In the early church, it was obvious that the Lord might manifest Himself and do extraordinary works through any believer at any time, but He did have leaders. Those leaders did not just have authority because they were appointed, but because the Lord was with them *to lead*. Peter boldly stepped beyond the present limits to preach the gospel on the Day of Pentecost and then to the Gentiles at the home of Cornelius. Because he followed the Lord, he repeatedly led the church in the new direction that the Lord wanted to go. The apostles were used to perform great miracles and even raised the dead. Leadership was not just a position; it was an action verb! Such was the nature of the apostolic ministry that laid the foundation in the first century, and we can expect the apostolic authority restored at the end to be like it.

It was also the nature of the apostolic leaders to recognize and support what the Lord did through any believer. When they heard that Samaria was receiving the word of the Lord through Phillip, they sent apostles to help lay a solid foundation in the believers there. When they heard that the Gentiles in Antioch had received the word, they sent Barnabas to help encourage and establish them. In this the leaders did not just lead, but followed the Holy Spirit and supported His ministry through whomever He chose to use.

However, the church was not recognized just by the apostles who ministered to her, but by the Lord Himself being among them. Like "the church in the wilderness," they followed the cloud by day and the pillar of fire by night. When He moved, so did they. When He stopped, they pitched a tent where He was. They only went where the presence of the Lord led them. They followed the Lamb, the living God, not just a formula. The temple of the Lord was built out of living stones. The church was recognized simply by the people He inhabited.

The first-century church exhibited a boldness that sent shockwaves throughout the world. This boldness cannot be explained by mere agreement with teachings. This boldness came from the living reality of Jesus in the midst of His people. Teaching was important, and the accuracy of their doctrine was firmly established by the Scriptures. Even so, they were not those who had just heard about the Lord, but those who followed Him. Their boldness was the result of the living God being in their midst. They grew in the knowledge of Him, but even more than that, they grew closer to Him. He was the reality of their lives.

The ultimate purpose of the Lord for every believer is that they become like Him and do the works that He did. His people are to be His witnesses, not because they have seen and known Him, but because He is with them now. It was the presence of the Lord, present tense, that gave the first-century church its dynamic authority to impact the world with the gospel, and it will be the same for the apostolic church that will be raised up again before the end comes. Our ultimate quest is to be a dwelling place for the Lord. This is the purpose of apostles and all of

WAR OF THE SOUL

the other ministries given to the church—to make us into His habitation.

To truly believe the testimony of Scripture is not to just believe that these things were done, but to have the faith to see them done through our own lives. To truly believe the Scriptures is witnessed by doing what is written in them. Anything less is the delusion of a religious spirit that will give glory to what God has done in order to justify neglecting or even persecuting what He is now doing.

When the real nature of apostolic Christianity is revealed again, it will expose every pretender. Like the early church, the last-day apostolic church can expect the worst persecution to come from those who claim to be Christians and who will claim vehemently to be the protectors of the truth. Good has always been the worst enemy of best, and those who have settled for a good thing will be the most offended when something better comes. This persecution helps to separate the wheat from the chaff.

Let us guard our hearts by humbling ourselves with the reality of just how far short we are now of the biblical stature of the church. We must rise above building our own little ministries if we are to be a part of building the true church. To build the true church, we must rise above preaching the church and preach the kingdom, which is the glorious person and domain of the King. It is His glory that we must seek, not our own, if we will again be apostolic.

APOSTOLIC TRAVAIL

In Galatians 4:19 Paul writes, **"My children, with whom I am again in labor until Christ is formed in you."** The apostolic travail Paul endured so that Christ would be formed in the church literally translated means "to be in pain." When the Lord called Paul, He said, **"For I will show him how much he must suffer for My name's sake" (Acts 9:16).** Later he was to write, **"For just as the sufferings of Christ are ours in abundance, so also our comfort is abundant through Christ (II Corinthians 1:5).** However, these were not just the sufferings of persecution, but they were the sufferings of a true spiritual parent who went through all of the pains of childbearing and rearing.

How people define their accomplishments reveals their true agendas. When I ask people about their work and they tell me how many churches they have started or how many people their television or radio programs reach, it is obvious that those are the most important things to them, which are certainly worthy causes. However, the Apostle Paul obviously measured his accomplishments by how the converts and churches he had been used to bring forth were becoming Christ-like. I only know a handful of Christian leaders today who would have this response, and I am not sure it would be mine, but I think it is the right one.

In modern Christianity, it can be easy to get caught up in the building of institutions, outreaches, or even buildings, but neglect the building of people. However, it is the people the Lord is looking at as His building. The early church may have had a large advantage by not having any buildings except public ones such as the temple, which they could occasionally use. However, used rightly, having buildings can be an aid to the work of equipping and raising up strong Christians. Buildings and even organizations must not be allowed to supplant our devotion to the people. The church is called to be a family first, not an organization. When we start becoming more of an organization than a family, we are losing our way.

THE ULTIMATE MEASURE OF A CHRISTIAN

Of course, the ultimate measure of Christians is how Christ-like they are in character and how effective they are in doing the works that He did. Because so many Christians have had embarrassing moral failures, there are perpetually those who are crying for character development over gifting. That sounds wise—only it does not seem to be the way the Lord did it. He gave remarkable power and authority to many throughout the Old and New Testaments who had serious character flaws and therefore failures. King David would be a good example in the Old Testament, but there are many others. In the New Testament, we could include all of His apostles. The night before the Lord was crucified, those apostles who were about to be the leaders of the church were fighting among themselves over who was the greatest. This was after sitting under the teaching and example of the greatest Leader there will ever be—Jesus.

It is easy to appreciate the "character-over-gifting" movements, but it is hard to find one that does not fall into a subtle but debilitating self-righteousness that can be more deadly than the moral failures some fall into. We must always remember that the Lord had almost unfathomable mercy for sinners but had no tolerance for the self-righteous. It was also the self-righteous who crucified Him because He did not come in a form that they expected or wanted. These are the ones who will rise up against those who do not fit into their own little categories, and the Lord almost always comes in those who will not fit neatly into our expectations.

We can see very clearly from the Scriptures what the Lord's moral standards are. It is a big mistake, which brings a clearly stated judgment, to compromise or promote their compromise in any way. We also see that He reserves an even greater judgment for the self-righteous, who parade their lack of failure as making them superior to those who have. This is a dilemma that is obviously meant to challenge every Christian. This was one of the primary conflicts in the first-century church, which we will spend a bit more time on later. We need to ask these questions: What would make the most righteous One to ever walk the earth so merciful? Why were sinners so attracted to Him, and why was He so obviously attracted to them, even to the point of calling some very questionable characters to be in the core leadership of His church?

This leads to another ultimate question: What does it mean to be "Christ-like?" The definition that most of us may believe is that He is most like what we want Him to be, but is this really what He is like? The severe tend to see Him as the Judge. Christians who are having problems and possibly trying to justify sin in their lives tend to see Him as the most merciful because that is what they need, but what is He really like?

Because He does not change, we know that He is not merciful one day and then harsh the next. He is consistent.

Paul exhorts us to **"behold then the kindness and severity of God"** (see Romans 11:22). Those who can only see His kindness but not His severity will be deceived, just as those who can only see His severity but not His kindness will be deceived. He is both, all of the time.

I am stating this here because being like Him is the ultimate measure of a Christian, but there is some confusion about what He is like. Church history can teach us much about this and should be one of the main understandings that we have as we study this history.

One thing that we know the apostles all ultimately agreed on was that love was the ultimate goal of Christian character. True love, which is God's love, is not just affection, but it is also severe at times and can even call for judgment. When it has been pressed to that point, it does so for the highest reasons, not out of impatience or rejection. So what would the church look like that has truly matured to demonstrate God's love? Can we find examples of it in history? If so, how did these churches achieve this? If not, what are the stumbling blocks to keep us from this ultimate demonstration of God's character?

But the goal of our instruction is love from a pure heart and a good conscience and a sincere faith (I Timothy 1:5).

This is one of those ultimate verses that can help keep us on course. The people and the church who keep their focus on growing in love for God and one another will stay on course and be the light in this world that they are called to be.

CHAPTER ELEVEN
JEWISH ROOTS AND GENTILE BRANCHES

We are taking our time to carefully examine the first-century church so that we can better understand what we are being restored to and the foundation that we are called to build upon.

THE SIGN

On the Day of Pentecost, the Spirit descended on the disciples, and they received the gift of tongues. As the Apostle Paul would later explain, this gift was given for "a sign." The sign that was given when the Spirit first came upon the church is obviously very important for us to understand, a key to which is found in Genesis 11:2-9. Now the whole earth used the same language and the same words.

> It came about as they journeyed east, that they found a plain in the land of Shinar and settled there.

> They said to one another, "Come, let us make bricks and burn them thoroughly." And

they used brick for stone, and they used tar for mortar.

They said, "Come, let us build for ourselves a city, and a tower whose top will reach into heaven, and let us make for ourselves a name, otherwise we will be scattered abroad over the face of the whole earth."

The LORD came down to see the city and the tower which the sons of men had built.

The LORD said, "Behold, they are one people, and they all have the same language. And this is what they began to do, and now nothing which they purpose to do will be impossible for them.

"Come, let Us go down and there confuse their language, so that they may not understand one another's speech."

So the LORD scattered them abroad from there over the face of the whole earth; and they stopped building the city.

Therefore its name was called Babel, because there the LORD confused the language of the whole earth; and from there the LORD scattered them abroad over the face of the whole earth.

In contrast to what happened at Babel, on the Day of Pentecost a gift was given so that for the first time since that infamous tower, all understood in a common language, as we see in Acts 2:5-12:

> Now there were Jews living in Jerusalem, devout men from every nation under heaven.
>
> And when this sound occurred, the crowd came together, and were bewildered because each one of them was hearing them speak in his own language.
>
> They were amazed and astonished, saying, "Why, are not all these who are speaking Galileans?
>
> "And how is it that we each hear them in our own language to which we were born?
>
> "Parthians and Medes and Elamites, and residents of Mesopotamia, Judea and Cappadocia, Pontus and Asia, Phrygia and Pamphylia, Egypt and the districts of Libya around Cyrene, and visitors from Rome, both Jews and proselytes,
>
> Cretans and Arabs—we hear them in our own tongues speaking of the mighty deeds of God."
>
> And they all continued in amazement and great perplexity, saying to one another, "What does this mean?"

This sign was a powerful statement that the church was to be the antithesis to the Tower of Babel where men's languages were scattered. Men from every nation and tongue would be gathered by the church to speak the only language that could ever truly unite men again—the message of the glory of God, which is realized through Jesus Christ.

Since that time we can look at history and say that the gospel has seemingly done more scattering than gathering. However, the Word of God is forever settled, and it will come to pass that when Jesus is truly lifted up—not the church, our doctrines, or our personalities—all men will be drawn to Him. He is the Word of God. The real Jesus is the desire of every human heart. Before the end of this age, we can count on the church to see Jesus as He is and present Him as He is so that the multitudes from every nation will come to Him.

When we look at the division within the church over the presentation of the gospel in the first century, and virtually every century since, it is easy to see why even Christians would tend to doubt that this kind of unity could ever be. Let us not forget that with the Lord a day is as a thousand years, and a thousand years are as a day (see II Peter 3:8). He can do in one day what we might think would take a thousand years. In due time, this unity will likely happen very swiftly. However, to prepare for it we must understand how the church departed so far from this. It is to understand matters such as this that we study church history. When we miss a turn and take the wrong road, it will not turn into the right road just because we have good intentions. We need to go back to where we missed the turn and get on the right road. That is called "repentance."

The Tower of Babel was man's most arrogant attempt to make a name for himself, to gather others around a project, and to reach heaven by his own strength. This is contrary to the plan of God that leads to redemption. He wants men to come to know His name, to gather around His Son, and to reach heaven the way that He has provided. The great sign that was given on the Day of Pentecost was to contrast what happened at Babel, a statement that unity would not be by man's might, power, or plans, but by the Spirit that was being given to them that day. The church would be God's tower to heaven, and it would gather men together again with a common purpose and a common language, which was the gospel of Jesus Christ.

The Wrong Turn

I once heard a man who had just moved to Atlanta say that he really appreciated those large signs that showed the way to Interstate 85, but he was just as thankful for the little ones that let him know that he was *still on* Interstate 85. God's signs are likewise given to show us the way and to keep us on the way. This first sign given on the day of the church's birth is crucial for us to follow. Only the Spirit can begat that which is Spirit. Only when Jesus is lifted up can men truly be gathered together. The things that the men of Babel vainly sought in the ways of their fallen nature reflects what God wants to do for men, but that only He can do. He wants to unite men, to give them a name, His name, and He does want them to reach into heaven and sit with Him on His throne. However, this can only be done by His Spirit.

After the first century, the church took a wrong turn and actually attempted what the men of Babel had tried to do. Instead of lifting up the name of Jesus, there was a subtle but perceptible drift toward lifting up the name of the church or individual leaders of the church. Then the church was presented as the mediator between God and men, which alone could unite men, but was in conflict with the Scripture which clearly states that Jesus alone is the only mediator between God and men (see I Timothy 2:5; Hebrews 8:6, 9:15,12:24). Ultimately, the church was presented as the way for men to reach heaven. This led to the divisions and scattering of men that remain to this day.

Whenever we try to gather men around any other project, regardless of how spiritual or good it seems, even if it is the church, it will ultimately result in men being even more scattered than before. If we are to stay on the right path, we must keep seeing the little signs along the way that are there to remind us of this most basic truth—that the church exists for the Lord, not the other way around. If the church is doing its job of lifting up Jesus, she will not be the center of attention—He will. If the temple is getting all of the attention, it is clear evidence that God is not in it—if He was, the church would not be getting the attention, regardless of how glorious the church is.

One can look at the history of the church and see many such towers built by human vanity that we have left in our wake. In the early Middle Ages, when the church was essentially united in this foolish task of trying to reach heaven by their own might and power, the Lord looked down on what they were building and again determined that the only remedy for this tragic folly was to scatter their languages. Now we have thousands of different spiritual languages, or denominations, movements, and anti-movements. Because of this, we will never be able to get together to finish such vain towers.

In later studies, we will examine in more detail just how this great departure from the course took place, as well as the attempts that the church has made to return to her first love and the true course. First, we need to look more closely at the first-century church so we can understand what we have departed from.

THE CRADLE OF THE CHURCH

The culture and conditions in which people are born and raised will inevitably have a profound impact on the development of their character and the paradigm from which they view life. Likewise, the culture in which the church was born was obviously intended by God to have had a significant influence on its development. The failure to understand the spiritual culture in which the church was born and raised for the first few years was a cause for some of her most devastating mistakes, many of which continue to this day.

The church was born and nurtured in the household of Judaism. Jesus was Jewish. The church was Jewish for the first seven years of its existence. The first apostles were all Jewish. The first disciples continued to follow the basic customs of Judaism. It has been said that a casual observer would have had trouble distinguishing the church from other Jewish sects of the time. In fact, the first apostles considered the church to be an extension of the nation of Israel rather than an entirely new faith for the first two decades of its existence.

Israel was the mother that carried and gave birth to the seed that became Christianity. This was God's purpose when He called Abraham and set aside a people for Himself. God married the mystical nation of Israel, and together they had a Son. This is the love story that permeates the Old Testament.

Even though this "mother" became hostile to her own children, the overreaction to this persecution from without and from the Judaisers within ended up doing more damage to the ultimate development of the church. The church's foundation was still intended to be Jerusalem, not Rome, which it gravitated toward after the severance with Judaism was made.

It was about twenty years after the birth of the church that converts began to consider a significant distinction between themselves and the Jewish nation. This was accomplished mostly through the emergence of a new breed of apostles led by Paul. The brilliant ministry and teachings of Paul helped to make it clear that men could become Christians without having to give themselves to the Old Covenant Law and rites. This is quite amazing since Paul had once been one of the most zealous of the strict Jewish sect, the Pharisees.

Paul's zeal for the traditions of Judaism had brought him into direct conflict with the truth of the gospel. This caused him to examine those traditions to a much greater degree than it seems any of the others had done. Paul's conversion had required that he be struck blind in the natural so that he could see in the Spirit and see the truth. This revolutionized his paradigm for viewing truth and ultimately resulted in the development of what is probably the greatest spiritual vision of all time. The most rigid, inflexible zealot became the greatest apostle of grace and laid the doctrine of the New Covenant more powerfully than any other. For this reason, Paul will forever be one of the greatest trophies of God's power of redemption.

Though Paul was healed of his blindness after three days, it took time for him to see clearly in the Spirit. As he wrote to the Galatians, he spent fourteen years alone with God in the wilderness searching these matters out. In some ways, this strengthened his understanding of the foundation of the gospel that was established in the Law and the Prophets. He was also able to see where the wrong understanding of the Law and Prophets caused the leaders of Israel to miss the time of their visitation, reject their Messiah, and oppose the truth just as he had. This was a strong foundation for his devotion to God's grace. It also enabled him to understand and have compassion for his Jewish brethren who were still trapped in the darkness that had once driven his life.

Like the unfolding of Paul's vision, the transition of the church, from being what was considered another Jewish sect to becoming a truly new creation, was a gradual process that unfolded over time. Even so, it is apparent that the break from its Jewish roots was never intended to be total. When Paul wrote to the Gentile church in Rome (the Book of Romans), it is considered the most comprehensive exposition of New Covenant theology in the Scriptures. Paul's explanation of the place of Israel in it (chapters 9-11) is a centerpiece of that theology. A departure from the warning he gives here became the reason for some of the church's greatest mistakes. We would do well to study these chapters in depth, but here I just want to direct your attention to the crucial verses in Romans 11:1-32:

> I say then, God has not rejected His people, has He? May it never be! For I too am an Israelite, a descendant of Abraham, of the tribe of Benjamin.

> God has not rejected His people whom He foreknew. Or do you not know what the Scripture says in the passage about Elijah, how he pleads with God against Israel?

> "Lord, they have killed Your prophets, they have torn down Your altars, and I alone am left, and they are seeking my life."

> But what is the divine response to him? "I have kept for Myself seven thousand men who have not bowed the knee to Baal."

> In the same way then, there has also come to be at the present time a remnant according to God's gracious choice.

But if it is by grace, it is no longer on the basis of works, otherwise grace is no longer grace.

What then? What Israel is seeking, it has not obtained, but those who were chosen obtained it, and the rest were hardened;

just as it is written, "God gave them a spirit of stupor, eyes to see not and ears to hear not, down to this very day."

And David says, "Let their table become a snare and a trap, and a stumbling block and a retribution to them.

"Let their eyes be darkened to see not, and bend their backs forever."

I say then, they did not stumble so as to fall, did they? May it never be! But by their transgression salvation has come to the Gentiles, to make them jealous.

Now if their transgression is riches for the world and their failure be riches for the Gentiles, how much more will their fulfillment be!

But I am speaking to you who are Gentiles. Inasmuch then as I am an apostle of Gentiles, I magnify my ministry,

if somehow I might move to jealousy my fellow countrymen and save some of them.

For if their rejection is the reconciliation of the world, what will their acceptance be but life from the dead?

If the first piece of dough be holy, the lump is also; and if the root be holy, the branches are too.

But if some of the branches were broken off, and you, being a wild olive, were grafted in among them and became partaker with them of the rich root of the olive tree,

do not be arrogant toward the branches; but if you are arrogant, remember that it is not you who supports the root, but the root supports you.

You will say then, "Branches were broken off so that I might be grafted in."

Quite right, they were broken off for their unbelief, but you stand by your faith. Do not be conceited, but fear;

for if God did not spare the natural branches, neither will He spare you, either.

Behold then the kindness and severity of God; to those who fell, severity, but to you, God's kindness, if you continue in His kindness; otherwise you also will be cut off.

And they also, if they do not continue in their unbelief, will be grafted in, for God is able to graft them in again.

For if you were cut off from what is by nature a wild olive tree, and were grafted contrary to nature into a cultivated olive tree, how much more will these who are the natural branches be grafted into their own olive tree?

For I do not want you, brethren, to be uninformed of this mystery—so that you will not be wise in your own estimation—that a partial hardening has happened to Israel until the fulness of the Gentiles has come in;

and so all Israel will be saved; just as it is written, "The Deliverer will come from Zion, He will remove ungodliness from Jacob."

"This is My covenant with them, when I take away their sins."

From the standpoint of the gospel they are enemies for your sake, but from the standpoint of God's choice they are beloved for the sake of the fathers;

for the gifts and the calling of God are irrevocable.

For just as you once were disobedient to God, but now have been shown mercy because of their disobedience,

so these also now have been disobedient, that because of the mercy shown to you they also may now be shown mercy.

For God has shut up all in disobedience so that He might show mercy to all.

Here we can see that God will never abandon His commitment to Israel. Even though the Jewish people were then enemies of the gospel (see verse 28), it was for the church's sake. A partial hardening had come upon the Jews to make them the greatest challenge to the gospel, which was done for the purpose of strengthening the gospel. It is the nature of true Christianity to thrive with opposition. The worst problems to ever confront the church have come when the world embraced and accepted the church.

As Paul explained to the Romans, the church was called to get so close to God that she would actually provoke the Jews to a godly jealousy so that they would be saved. If the church could reach the Jews, who had been made especially hard to reach, then the church could reach the whole world. It was for this reason that the church was exhorted to preach to the Jews first, not just in favoritism, but because the ability of their message to reach the Jews was the "acid test" of whether they had the truth. It was clearly the Lord's intention to restore **"the natural branches"** (**see verses 22-32**), and to do it through the Gentiles.

The Gentiles have received the blessings of the Scriptures and the Messiah through the Jewish people. The Jewish people will receive the blessing of the gospel through the Gentiles. All are in need of mercy, and all will receive it, including the Jewish people, who rejected their own Messiah. God gives His grace to the humble (see James 4:6). It took humility for the Gentiles to receive their grace through the Jewish people, and it will take humility for the Jewish people to receive their grace through the Gentiles.

The most important prophets, kings, and spiritual movements are inevitably born in difficult, hostile conditions. God's ways are contrary to fallen man's ways. His wisdom is far above the greatest human wisdom, but can only be seen through the eyes of true humility, which are like a child's eyes. What happened to Judaism to make it oppose the very One that they had waited so many centuries for also happened to Christianity when it "matured," causing the institutional church to one day become an even greater persecutor of truth than Judaism had been. The same evil has been able to creep into every fresh spiritual movement so that it would in turn persecute the next spiritual generation.

Instead of the church seeing the hardened Jews as a challenge to test the quality of their own life and message, the increasingly Gentile church gradually abandoned the commission to go to the Jews first. After the destruction of Jerusalem, the spiritual center of the church gradually moved west until it was centered in Rome and Constantinople. As this happened, all ties to Judaism were severed. Paul's warning not to become arrogant toward the natural branches was forgotten. He had warned that this would result in them being cut off from the root also. This happened as the life and power of the Holy Spirit was gradually substituted with rituals that were foreign to both Judaism and the apostles.

CHAPTER TWELVE

THE LAW PROPHESIED

The early church had a profound devotion to the Scriptures, basing all of their teachings and their prophetic perspectives on them. This was basic Jewish culture at the time, as it was the custom of the Jews to always search the Scriptures to verify important events. Only when they saw them verified by the Scriptures would they readily embrace them as having been from God. This had been their practice for hundreds of years. Even hundreds of years later, Mohammed, the founder of Islam, would call them "the people of the book." The first-century church was likewise unwavering in this devotion. They also had the remarkable example of how Jesus, the Word Himself, even when He had been tempted by the devil, took His stand on "It is written!"

The church was called to be the possession of God, His dwelling place. The Law had been given to prepare His people for this. However, it did not prepare them by making them righteous and holy, because by the time the church was born, it was apparent to many of the unbelieving Jews that "the letter" could not do this, so they turned to other rituals such as baptisms. However, the Law did prepare the people by revealing the standards of God's righteousness and holiness. Because we are unrighteous and unholy, we cannot measure up to them. Therefore, we desperately need His salvation and His power in order to live a holy life. The Law compels us to flee to the cross for salvation.

It is obvious that the first Christians saw the cross as more than the place of forgiveness, but as a means of deliverance and power that we might live righteous and holy before Him. The cross does not just extend forgiveness and then leave us in our sins. The cross is also the power of God to live rightly before Him, which the Law did not have. This basic truth is the reason why Paul wrote the Book of Galatians, as well as some of the other great New Testament expositions.

Even so, there is another purpose for the Law which was grasped by the early church as well. In Matthew 5:18, the Lord made a statement about this purpose for the Law: **"For truly I say to you, until heaven and earth pass away, not the smallest letter or stroke shall pass away from the Law *until all is accomplished*."** He is not saying here that the Law would not pass away until we have kept all of the commandments, because that would be in conflict with the basic principles of the New Covenant. He was explaining that the Law's purpose in being a *prophecy*. He also affirmed them in Matthew 11:13 when He said: **"For all the prophets and *the Law prophesied* until John."**

Not only did it prophesy of the coming of Christ, but it contains in remarkable detail an outline of history.

In His great wisdom, the Lord knew and foretold even the mistakes that the church would make, her apostasy, as well as her glorious recovery and conclusion at the end of the age.

All of the rituals and feasts of the Law prophetically portrayed Christ. That is why both the Lord Jesus and the early church continued to observe them. This was not done for righteousness because they well understood that their righteousness was gained through the cross alone. However, the first-century church continued to observe the rituals of the Law as a celebration of the reality of what they had now become since they were fulfilled in Christ. When the church was completely cut off from its Jewish roots, pagan rituals were substituted for those that truly spoke of Christ, and the drift toward deep darkness ensued.

Modern Christians often forget that the Old Testament was the only Bible that the first-century church had and that it was the foundation for the New Testament doctrines of the faith. The apostles used the Law and the Prophets to prove their revelation of the kingdom of God and to prove that Jesus was the promised Messiah, as we see in the text below:

Now to Him who is able to establish you according to my gospel and the preaching of Jesus Christ, according to the revelation of the mystery which has been kept secret for long ages past,

but now is manifested, and by the Scriptures of the prophets, according to the commandment

of the eternal God, has been made known to all the nations, leading to obedience of faith (Romans 16:25-26).

When they had set a day for Paul, they came to him at his lodging in large numbers; and he was explaining to them by solemnly testifying about the kingdom of God and trying to persuade them concerning Jesus, from both the Law of Moses and from the Prophets, from morning until evening (Acts 28:23).

"The Scriptures" that Paul refers to in Romans 16 and in all of his other letters are what we call the Old Testament, because at that time they did not have the New Testament. In fact, they were writing it! Again, the Old Testament was the only Bible that the early church had, and it was the basis for all of their doctrines and practices, including their revelation of the grace of God through Christ.

We tend to think of the Old Testament as Law and the New Testament as Grace, but this is not necessarily true. The Old Covenant is "the letter;" the New Covenant is lived by faith through the Holy Spirit. If you read the New Testament with an Old Covenant heart, it will be just Law to you. Likewise, if you read the Old Testament with a New Covenant heart, you will see Christ in all of it.

The terminology used in the New Testament to describe the place and ministry of the Lord Jesus is from the terminology used in the Law and the Prophets. He is called the High Priest after the Old Testament type, who was the mediator between the nation of Israel and the Lord. He is called "the Lamb of God" after the sacrificial lamb that, according to the Law, was to atone for the sins of the people. That is why Jesus made the astonishing statement in John 5:46-47:

> "For if you believed Moses, you would believe Me; for he wrote of Me.
>
> "But if you do not believe his writings, how will you believe My words?"

He made a similar statement in Luke 24:25-27:

> And He said to them, "O foolish men and slow of heart to believe in all that the prophets have spoken!
>
> "Was it not necessary for the Christ to suffer these things and to enter into His glory?"
>
> Then beginning with Moses and with all the prophets, He explained to them the things concerning Himself in all the Scriptures.

We will indeed be foolish if we do not believe *all* that is written in the Law and Prophets. A considerable amount of the foolishness that the church has fallen to can be attributed to our failure in this. We, too, need to keep in mind the exhortation that Paul gave in II Timothy 3:14-17:

> You, however, continue in the things you have learned and become convinced of, knowing from whom you have learned them,

and that from childhood you have known the sacred writings which are able to give you the wisdom that leads to salvation through faith which is in Christ Jesus.

All Scripture is inspired by God and profitable for teaching, for reproof, for correction, for training in righteousness;

so that the man of God may be adequate, equipped for every good work.

Of course, the **"all Scripture"** that Paul is referring to here is what we call the Old Testament. The Law and the Prophets, which was the only Bible the early church had, was enough to cause them to turn the world upside down. Now we have the New Testament also. The Lord really did save His best wine for last. Even so, the addition of the New Testament was never meant to supplant the purpose of that which we call the Old Testament.

It should be noted that the writer of what is considered the meatiest of the New Testament Epistles, the Book of Hebrews, lamented that he could only give the readers milk because they were not ready for solid food! This Book contains information about Melchizedek, the tabernacle, an expansive overview of the purposes of God, all of which were still spiritual milk and not solid food! This should give us great cause for humility. How many Christians today even know what the Melchizedek priesthood is? That is the priesthood that we are called to in Christ, so is it not time that we get weaned from milk and go on to solid food? Much of that solid food is found in the Old Testament, which can only be seen when it is understood as a prophecy.

ROOT AND BRANCHES

Now how does all of this apply to the distinction between the Jewish and Gentile churches? First, we need to see God's purpose for keeping them distinct and yet one in Christ. Even though they were to be different in many ways, it was the obvious intention of the Lord for the Gentile "branches" of the church to be linked to the Jewish "roots," as Paul explained in Romans. Even so, the Gentile "branches" were allowed to establish a church life that was profoundly different from Jewish Christians. This was done with the full blessing and encouragement of the original apostles, verified by the Holy Spirit, and established by the Scriptures. The first council in Jerusalem (see Acts 15) confirmed this and liberated the Gentiles from all of the rituals of the Law, concluding with the following:

> **"For it seemed good to the Holy Spirit and to us to lay upon you no greater burden than these essentials:**
>
> **"that you abstain from things sacrificed to idols and from blood and from things strangled and from fornication; if you keep yourselves free from such things, you will do well. Farewell"** (Acts 15:28-29).

It is often overlooked that this decree was issued specifically for Gentiles and not for Jewish believers.

Jewish believers were obviously free to continue observing the rituals contained in the Law and Prophets, not for righteousness' sake, which could alone come through the cross of Jesus, but they did this to honor their heritage. As stated, these were not kept as a celebration but rather for righteousness, as the Epistle to the Hebrews makes clear. However, it is important for us to see that a distinction is made between what was required of the Jewish and Gentile believers.

A primary stumbling block that keeps many from being able to see this is the concept that Judaism only represented the keeping of the Law for righteousness, which nullifies the grace that we receive through Christ. Many of the first Jewish believers, as well as even some of the Gentile believers, also had a hard time making this distinction. Even so, it seems to be the clear intent of the Holy Spirit for the Jewish believers to keep alive the prophetic rituals and celebrations, and the Gentile church to develop a style that was completely fresh and new. As long as the Jewish and Gentile believers were linked in fellowship, the important moorings of the church in the historic path of God's redemptive purposes through Israel would be maintained through the Jewish roots of the church.

Another fact that made it clear that the Lord intended for there to be a distinction between the Gentile and Jewish believers was the appointment of an apostle to the Jews and an apostle to the Gentiles. It is significant that Paul referred to the Gentile "branches" (plural), which indicated that there would be diversity within the Gentile groups.

With strong moorings to the Jewish roots, there could be a considerable liberty in the expression of the faith through different cultures and races, while still maintaining knowledge of God's righteousness and holiness. With the fresh, creative vitality of the Gentile branches, the Jewish roots would not be as prone to fall back into the rigid inflexibility of the Law. Both are essential, but they had to remain linked to each other while being free to be unique and different.

God, who loves diversity so much that He makes every snowflake different, who delighted in making people so different, obviously intended from the beginning for the church to reflect His glorious creativity. Even so, in Christ we are also to become **"one new man" (see Ephesians 2:15)**. Understanding the **"one new man"** in this light has been difficult because we tend to only be able to see unity in conformity instead of the higher unity in diversity. A man does not become one with his wife by making her a man but by appreciating the differences of the woman. Likewise, the Jewish and Gentile churches must learn to appreciate the intended differences to come into a true unity in Christ. When this is truly accomplished, it will be a remarkable demonstration of God's will for the unity of all nations through His Son, which is exactly what it will be when it is accomplished at the end of this age.

This is why Paul so resolutely preached that even though the Jews had been hardened to the gospel, they would be grafted in again as "natural branches" (see Romans 11:28-32). This is why the modern Messianic

Jewish congregations now spreading around the world are so important. Though both the Messianic and Gentile congregations of today are still far from the apostolic model of the first century, they are both moving toward what was intended in the beginning and confirmed by the council in Jerusalem. At the end, this **"one new man"** will be composed of those from every nation.

When this unity between Jew and Gentile is accomplished, it will represent the overcoming of the ultimate racist barriers in the church. Such grace can only come through humility on the part of both the Jews and the Gentiles, which enables each to clearly see the purposes of God for the other. Because God gives His grace to the humble, this will enable the releasing of unprecedented power to His people, even the power that raises the dead.

NEXT YEAR IN JERUSALEM?

The overreaction to Judaism by the early church is understandable in the light of three main factors. The first was the persecution that the young church endured from traditional Judaism. Second were the problems caused by Jewish converts who tried to impose the Law on the Gentile believers. The third was the destruction of Jerusalem in 70 A.D. When Jerusalem was destroyed, it scattered the remaining Jewish apostles and elders, severing most of the links that the Gentile churches had with their Jewish brethren.

At the end of this age, we are seeing all of these conditions being reversed. The nation of Israel has been regathered, and Jerusalem has again been repossessed by the Jewish people. Multitudes of Messianic Jewish congregations are forming around the world and throughout the land of Israel. We will soon see Jerusalem again become a spiritual center of the faith, just as many biblical prophecies declare. At the end, the church will again be restored to its strong Jewish roots and will also have strong Gentile branches.

Even so, for the true unity that God desires between the Gentile branches and the Jewish roots, neither will have to compromise their uniqueness. When the joining is right, each will be free to be who God has called them to be. Then the church will truly be a **"house of prayer for all the nations" (see Mark 11:17)**, or, literally, "a house of prayer for all ethnic groups."

CHAPTER THIRTEEN
EARLY CHURCH GOVERNMENT

In the previous chapters, we examined the message and lifestyle of the first-century church, as well as a brief overview of its spiritual culture. In this chapter, we will view the church government established by the apostles.

THE GOVERNMENT OF LIBERTY

Church government under the original apostles was so unique, free, and yet effective that it defies definition. Like the other great principles of the faith, if it is overly defined, the essence of what it is intended to be will be lost. The first-century church government was not dependent on the form, but on the anointing of the leaders who held the positions in it. Because of this, authority in the church was defined more by the ones leading it than by the system of government because the church was not built on a form, but rather on people.

This is in contrast to our civil governments, which need a high degree of definition because they are not trying to lead people who are necessarily in pursuit of God and His righteousness. Because of this, civil governments tend to be very legalistic or based on laws more than on specific leaders. Not just the government, but the culture in the United States has evolved into probably the most legalistic society in the world. This is highlighted by the fact that it has many times the number of lawyers that other modern nations have, and now nearly every transaction is done with a contract that is many times the size of what one would expect just because of the legal language involved. This has become a major stranglehold not only on enterprise, but in almost every aspect of life—sometimes driving the cost into multiples of what they would be otherwise. The reason for this is that we have "lawmakers" in positions of leadership, who are mostly lawyers and whose mentality is to respond to any situation or crisis with laws and regulations rather than leading and managing through them.

For this reason, our "leaders" tend to view the answer to a crisis as the need for new regulations or laws. These laws are so stacked on top of one another that the laws themselves are now the cause of great crises. Certainly laws and regulations are needed, and some of our problems have resulted from not having needed regulation, but the overreaction has been at least as damaging as the original problems—maybe even more so. The present mentality of the U.S. Government to meet every need or problem with laws and regulations is causing the most prosperous, powerful, and advanced society on earth to collapse under the weight of them.

I'm using the previous as an example, but the spiritual authority of the church is intended to be very different. When churches become legalistic in the nature of their leadership, they likewise tend to respond to every problem with a new rule, and they bog down under the weight of them so that there is little or no hope of actually responding to the leadership of the Holy Spirit. The first-century church was governed by a very different mentality than this. Their leaders led through crisis. Having been under the yoke of the Old Covenant, they were very reticent to make any rules or regulations for the church. Their answer to problems was to train and raise up elders who had the wisdom and courage to lead as judges in the church and who were capable of judging situations and disputes.

The apostles did not even have a constitution which decreed that they could dictate policy. Their authority came from something much higher—they had been with Jesus, and they were anointed by Him. Their exercise of authority was both hierarchical and democratic. Their main function was to lay a solid foundation of doctrine and to establish a church government that promoted liberty, not conformity. They did this very well. The freedom this allowed enabled the hearts of men to be converted by the power of truth, not just by coercion.

The adherence of the apostles to this course of leadership was in such contrast to anything that had been known before, and certainly to the culture of the times, that it constitutes the most extraordinary leadership ever exercised by any government at any time. Under this form of government, the church was able to be responsive to the Holy Spirit in situations and crises. As the church drifted from the genius of this extraordinary style of leadership, oppression grew. The power of truth was replaced with a terrible, barbaric force intended to compel men to bend their knees to the dictates of church leaders without bending their hearts to the truth.

When the church began the long process of returning to its original form of church government, the birth of democracy in civil governments and the esteem for human dignity and liberty for all were the immediate results. The true freedom movements of the last five hundred years can all be traced to the teachings of the Reformation leaders. Without question, religious liberty is the foundation upon which all true liberty will be based. Most democratic governments will drift into the bondage of legalism mentioned if they are not led by true leaders. The civil freedom that is enjoyed almost anywhere in the world today can be traced to the freedom by which Christ set His people free.

With freedom comes responsibility. It was for the purpose of freedom that the Lord placed the Tree of the Knowledge of Good and Evil in the Garden. It was not to cause Adam and Eve to fall, but to give them freedom so that they could prove their obedience and faithfulness to the Lord. There can be no true obedience unless there is the freedom to disobey. This is why the gospel is sent out with such humility, carried by earthen vessels.

In this age, the Lord is calling forth a people to be joint heirs with Him. They will rule and reign with Him over the nations. He will only have in this great position those who came because they loved the truth, not just out of political expediency or a lust for power. These will prove their love for the truth by taking their stand for righteousness when it is least expedient, even to the forfeiture of their lives if that is what is required. These will not have come out of compulsion, but something much deeper—hearts that love God and His ways above all else. The first Eve lived in a perfect world and chose to sin. The bride of the last Adam will have lived in a most evil world but will choose to obey. Such alone are worthy to be the bride of the Lamb.

THE FORMS OF GOVERNMENT

Even though God's government is based more on the authority and leadership He has brought forth in His people, there has to be some form of government for there to be government. In the first-century church, we actually see different forms of government. This concept is so foreign to most people's perspectives that even many church historians failed to see this. However, the early church actually had different forms of government that seem to be especially related to different situations and possibly even cultures the churches were raised up in. This was indeed another form of genius in government.

Many are repelled by the abuses of hierarchies in church government. Even though this form of government has been used to stifle liberty in the church, it was an aspect of New Testament church government. Councils of apostles and elders were the ultimate earthly manifestation of church government, and in each one there was a presiding leader. However, one can also use the New Testament to make a case for having co-equal elders as a government for the church. Both forms of government have merits and biblical precedents. What we cannot say is that either form is *the* New Testament form of church government. It seems that even in the form of church government that we use, the Lord intended for us to have liberty and diversity. This can seem impractical to the natural mind, but for true spiritual development, it is essential.

Even the best form of government will be bad government without good people in it. Likewise, the worst form of government can be good government if it has good people in it. If we want good government, we cannot over-emphasize the form. Nevertheless, our goal should be to have good, qualified people in leadership, with the best form of government that will be an aid and not a hindrance to the anointing of that particular group.

As we read the New Testament, it seems as if the form of church government used just evolved over time. This is an accurate depiction. Again, the Lord was building His government around people, not trying to build people around a form of government. This is not to imply that the Lord did not know where He was going with this. However, when too much government is imposed on people prematurely, it can stifle true spiritual development—especially leadership development.

On the other hand, when a group is young, they will probably need more control than when they are mature. This is a delicate balance, and there will certainly be a temptation to just impose what brings control. However, if we are truly wise, we will be careful, patient, and flexible in imposing a government on a new church or movement. In this way, the anointing that is in the people can give definition to the government.

The Lord almost always works from the inside out, not the outside in. If our overwhelming emphasis is on imposing a form of government and getting the church to fit into it, at best we are going to end up causing a lot of pain. Government is important. One of the great evils of the last days is lawlessness. Even so, how the government is imposed can be a great help or hindrance to the work. Some people need much more structure in church government than others, and we have the liberty in the New Testament to build this way. When less structure is needed, we also have that liberty.

The New Testament church government was intended to be flexible enough to change as the church grows. People who have lived under oppressive forms of government, such as communism or fascism, can have their own "decision makers" so broken or under-developed that too much liberty can be destructive and confusing to their walks in the Lord if it is not released to them gradually. In recent history, we saw this also take place in Russia when the yoke of communism was broken—the people were suddenly free, but really did not know how or were not able to handle this freedom. Quickly the Russian mafia filled the vacuum, and the lawlessness was viewed by many as much worse than the yoke of communism. A leadership then arose that wisely reapplied many restraints so that freedom could be gradually given to the people at a pace they could handle.

In countries where liberty is deep and cultural, almost any exercise of church authority will be viewed as an imposition of a control spirit. This will cause serious rebellions that could have been avoided if needed authority would have been taken more gradually. In places where there has been a good balance between liberty and control (not a control spirit), very little government may be needed.

In all cases, church government is intended to help us grow in our submission to the Headship of Jesus. Our goal should always be to promote the individual's personal relationship to the Lord, ability to know His voice, and commitment to follow Him, so that every one of God's people has the law written in his or her hearts. If we do not keep this ultimate goal in mind, our form of government will fail, regardless of what form it is. This was the true pattern that was left to us by the first-century apostles.

The Realms of Authority

Basic to the teachings of the early church is that Jesus is the Head of His church. There is no other leader on earth that can presume that position. He alone is *the* authority over the entire church. The apostles were the first appointed officers of the church, and they were its highest authority on earth. However, apostolic authority was not universal. Paul explained this when he wrote to the Corinthians, **"If to others I am not an apostle, at least I am** to you; for you are the seal of my apostleship in the Lord" (I Corinthians 9:2). He is saying by this that he was not an apostle to everyone, but he was to them because they were a fruit of his apostolic anointing.

When Paul went to Jerusalem, he was honored as an apostle to the Gentiles, but he was not received as an apostle to the Jews, and he did not try to exercise apostolic authority in Jerusalem. In some places we can be received as an apostle and in others maybe just as a teacher, just as a pastor over one congregation cannot impose his pastoral authority over other congregations. We must recognize the limits of our authority in every situation and stay within them. If we do not, our rejection will not be the result of hard-hearted people as much the result of our own presumptions.

Likewise, Peter was not an apostle to the Gentiles, even though he was used to open the door of the gospel to them. When he went to the Gentiles at Antioch, he got into trouble, and Paul, who was called to the Gentiles, had to rebuke him. That Paul, one of the youngest apostles at the time and not even one of the twelve, had the author-ity to do this, and that Peter submitted to it, is truly a remarkable demonstration of how church government at the time worked. Obviously, Paul had more authority in Antioch than Peter did.

It also seems that Peter had this failure of judgment and action because he was no longer in his realm of authority. When we leave our realm of authority, we depart from the realm of grace that we have been given. Peter just did not have the grace to minister among the Gentiles because he was called to the Jews.

Likewise, when Paul went to the Jews in Jerusalem, he got into trouble. This is hard for some to accept because Paul is almost worshiped as infallible, but there was an easier way for him to go to Rome than in chains. It seems that the Holy Spirit repeatedly tried to warn him not to go to Jerusalem. Certainly a good argument can also be made for Paul's having done the will of the Lord by going to Jerusalem, but I personally believe that it was a mistake on his part not to heed those warnings. Regardless, the principle is still true—that apostles have realms of authority. If we go beyond those realms, we have gone beyond the grace that we have been given, and we will have troubles.

It is important to reiterate the point that even though Peter was used to open the door of faith to the Gentiles, he was not called to them. Just because we are used to start something does not mean that we have authority there. When Mary, the mother of Jesus, came to Him, He responded that His mother, brothers, and sisters were those who did the will of God. He was saying this to let it be known that just because she gave birth to Him, it did not mean that she had the right to control Him. Not understanding this one point about spiritual authority has caused considerable trouble for the church. When we become possessive, we will probably depart from our appointed realms of authority.

APOSTOLIC GOVERNMENT

Some have the concept that the ultimate unity of the church can only come from being under one church government. This is both a superficial and dangerous concept. We will not come into our ultimate unity until we all come under the Headship of Jesus, but the true unity will be a unity in diversity, not a unity of conformity, especially in church government.

Numerous apostolic movements are now being raised up around the world. Most are very unique, which is a testimony to their authenticity. One of the banes of modern Christianity has been the tendency of unanointed people to try to gain influence and followers in the church by being able to copy other anointed people. Living water only comes out of the innermost being, the heart. Parrots may be able to copy what we say, but it is not in their hearts. A true apostolic movement, or government, must come from what the Lord has deposited in the heart of the apostle, not by his ability to copy others well. This is especially true as it relates to church government.

When true unity comes, all of the apostolic movements will appreciate the uniqueness of the others, embracing a proper level of interchange, but not feeling compelled to be like others. We must have uniqueness if we are ever going to be the body of Christ that we have been called to be. If we are going to be such a body, we do not need to all be hands, eyes, or any other part. We need to each be unique and different but function together.

In the first century, all authority in the church was derived from the apostles. This was hierarchical, regardless of how much we may want to resist that principle. Even so, the way in which they exercised their authority was to transfer it to any worthy subordinates at every opportunity. Authority was not considered a position of privilege as much as a responsibility to be used for service.

When the position of deacon was instituted, the apostles allowed the congregation to choose those who were to serve with this honor. Regardless of how we would like to view this, it was a remarkable example of democracy in church government. Just as Peter later wrote, the apostles did not act as if they were lords of God's inheritance, but that they were led by being examples to the flock (see I Peter 5:3). They took authority when it was needed, but they seemed to be devoted to delegating it to the people when possible. If these people were to one day rule over angels, should they not be able to take responsibility in earthly matters?

TEAM MINISTRY

The apostles in the first century were established by the Lord, but as they laid a foundation in the church with their teaching and leadership, other ministries began to emerge. Each of these specialized in an aspect of the apostolic ministry. The apostles were all prophets, evangelists, pastors, and teachers, at least to some degree. The emerging ministries from the church all seemed to specialize in just one or two of these ministries. Some focused on evangelism, others teaching, others the prophetic, administration, healing, and so on. In this way, the ministry that had begun with twelve grew throughout the expanding church, meeting the expanding needs. The Holy Spirit that was given to each one brought forth gifts and ministries in each, so that every believer had a part in the overall ministry of the church.

We read in the Book of Acts that it seems all of this happened quite swiftly, but actually it took many years to unfold. For example, it was seven years from the day that the Holy Spirit was poured out on Pentecost until Peter first preached to the Gentiles in the house of Cornelius. It was over two decades from the outpouring of the Holy Spirit until Paul and Barnabas were sent out from Antioch.

This unfolding definition of the church is a good pattern for church life if it is not artificial. When you have a baby, you may know that it is male or female, but you really will not know what he or she will look like until adulthood. The same is true of the church. For centuries, unfolding movements in the church have often been subject to being made to try to fit into the clothes that were made for them before they were even born, rather than having the wisdom to wait and make the clothes to fit the child.

As stated, throughout the Lord's ministry on earth, He only made a couple of brief mentions of the church and gave very little definition to what it would be like. Even though He spent many days after His resurrection sharing about the kingdom with His disciples, it seems that He actually gave them very little practical guidance concerning the administration of the church. It is obvious that He purposely wanted them to get that from the Holy Spirit.

The Holy Spirit seemed to only give wisdom as they needed it, so the structure of the church unfolded over time. In this way, the brilliance of what unfolded was far beyond human genius, and it perfectly fit the needs at each stage of development. It may have been much simpler to just impose an unyielding model of government in the beginning, but it would not have been nearly as effective.

As the ministries emerged, a comprehensive team began to form. Prophets began to work closely with the apostles. The pastors and teachers worked closely together. The only evangelist mentioned in the New Testament, Philip, seemed to work alone, but apostles were sent to follow up his work. Local elders were appointed in each congregation to provide guidance and protection in the absence of the apostles, which was most of the time. Together this structure of leadership and responsibility represented an innovation in organization such as the world had never seen. It soon became so powerful that its very existence challenged the existence of the most powerful institutions and governments on earth.

There were times when the apostles dictated policy or took severe action against sin or false doctrines that encroached on the church. We have a number of these examples in the New Testament Epistles. Even so, when we see Paul issuing instructions for disciplinary action to the Corinthian church, he did not just address the elders, but rather the entire congregation. Basically, the apostles treated believers as if they were fellow heirs of the kingdom, kings and priests to God. All believers were therefore treated with the utmost respect. Even so, clear lines of authority were established in the first-century church, as we see in see I Corinthians 12:27-31:

> **Now you are Christ's body, and individually members of it.**

> **And God has appointed in the church, first apostles, second prophets, third teachers, then miracles, then gifts of healings, helps, administrations, various kinds of tongues.**

> **All are not apostles, are they? All are not prophets, are they? All are not teachers, are they? All are not workers of miracles, are they?**

> **All do not have gifts of healings, do they? All do not speak with tongues, do they? All do not interpret, do they?**

> **But earnestly desire the greater gifts. And I show you a still more excellent way.**

Here we see a clear chain of authority, and yet the believers are exhorted to desire the greater gifts. They are reminded that all do not have the same authority but that they could seek more of it. However, we must keep in mind that the basic mentality of leadership and authority in the first century was to be a servant, so seeking more authority was to seek to be a greater servant of all.

They also had the great example of how the Lord had called Paul from being one of the greatest enemies of the church to being one of its greatest leaders. The Lord seemed to delight in using His leaders as demonstrations of His power of redemption. The small and the weak, even the base, were often the ones the Lord wanted to use (see I Corinthians 1:26-29). A main purpose of God for the church was to be an instrument through which He could reach to redeem and restore the lost. Those who were the most in touch with redemption and restoration were the most qualified to carry authority in His church.

ELDERS

The elders were the highest local authority in a church. This office was borrowed from Israel's government that had been established by Moses in the wilderness. In Israel, there were basically two classes of elders. Because of the Law's admonition to honor fathers and mothers, as well as other biblical exhortations to respect the aged, all of the elderly were given honor and influence in the affairs of the community. However, just as Moses chose seventy elders **"from among the elders" (see Numbers 11:16)** to exercise governing authority, governing elders in the church were distinguished from those who were simply due respect for their age and faithfulness.

After Israel entered the Promised Land and possessed cities to live in, a primary responsibility of the governing elders was to sit in the gates of the city. Here they acted as judges, determining who would be allowed to come in or go out of the city. Each gate into the city had a different function. Some were for the merchants to use, others for the soldiers, or nobility, and so forth. Each elder could exercise authority over different aspects of the city's life because of the gate that he sat in.

This has an important application in the New Testament. Because elders are always mentioned as plural, it can be assumed that elders are always intended to function in plurality. Some have assumed that plurality implies that elders were all equal in authority, but both the Old Testament and New Testament examples indicate that this is not the case. Elders who sat in one gate did not have the authority to dictate policy over other gates. These may seem like small points, but their application in the church can have major consequences.

For example, if we choose someone to be an elder because of his maturity or the respect that he has in the community of believers, but he has not been given a specific function, he could easily become a hindrance to the progress of the church, even if he has the best of intentions. Before someone is appointed a "governing elder," we should look for the evidence of God's anointing on him. In the case of Moses, the Spirit came upon them and they prophesied. This may not be exactly how the Lord verifies every elder, but we need to recognize the Spirit upon the person for government. If we appoint someone to this position just to honor him, we will probably pay a high price for it later.

Another important point here is to determine just what "gate" the governing elders are called to sit at. Should one who is anointed to oversee the deacons have authority over the children's ministry, where they may have no anointing or experience? It seems that a modern example of what the presbytery of the church is intended to be like is our Presidential Cabinet. For example, heads of the different departments of government sit in a council. The Secretary of Defense may have some wisdom for the Department of Labor, but he does not have the authority to dictate policy there. Elders may have wisdom for other ministries in the church, but one who is an overseer of one "gate," or ministry, should not be able to dictate authority over someone else's sphere of authority.

Of course, important doctrinal issues may arise that involve the entire church, such as we see in Acts 15. This required a council of all of the apostles and elders. After listening to testimonies and debate, James, who was recognized as the leading elder in Jerusalem, made the decisive statement to decide the issue (see verses 13-19). Since this **"seemed good" (see Acts 15:22)** to the other apostles and elders, a decree was issued concluding the council.

Another sphere of authority for elders can be tied to geography. When Paul talked about his sphere of authority, it was in relation to geographical boundaries (see II Corinthians 10:13-16). Because the Lord established cultures, races, and nations, He obviously prepares special ministries to relate to them. Likewise, there should be a sensitivity to these that everyone in ministry needs. This was why Paul said that when he was in Rome, he did like the Romans, or when he was with the Jews, he became as a

Jew. We do not want our personalities to become *unnecessary* stumbling blocks to the gospel. Many of the unnecessary offenses to Christianity have come because we have failed to walk in this wisdom or have tried to go beyond the realm of authority that was given to us geographically.

We should also recognize that when Peter and John referred to themselves as elders, they were not talking about being elders in a local church or even in the foundational church of Jerusalem. Peter and John were both recognized as elders of the whole body of Christ. Does this not conflict with the statement that the Lord alone is Head of the whole church? No, it does not. Some realms of authority are international, and some may even extend to the whole church.

Today we could include a few in this position who have international respect and influence as leaders, and not just because their television programs are carried internationally. At one time, Billy Graham was voted the most influential man in America, even though he held no public office. However, the respect for him was such that if he communicated respect for someone else, or something else, he or she was immediately respected and gained stature in the eyes of just about everyone, even the heathen. Likewise, John Calvin was not even a citizen of Geneva and never held a public office, but no law was passed without his approval. It was not an official authority but one that was much greater—spiritual authority, which was based on the merit of his character.

Being respected in such a capacity does not give one the authority to dictate policy over the entire church, but these men have been seated or are beginning to sit at gates, or spiritual doors, which are releasing something into the entire church. Many others have international ministries. Though some of them may have both age and longevity in those positions, they just do not carry the kind of authority that would cause us to recognize them as elders of the entire body of Christ.

Biblically and throughout church history, we can recognize elders on the local church level and on the international level, but does this mean that we can have elders positioned on levels in-between these? To be a biblical people does not mean that we cannot do anything unless we find it specifically written in the Scriptures; rather it means that we have the liberty to do it if it does not specifically violate what is written. This does not mean that anything we do that does not violate Scripture is right, but that we are free to be led by the Holy Spirit in these matters. I personally think that it is right to recognize elders on every level of authority that we are ministering in, which would include recognizing elders in specific positions within movements.

Was there meant to be a hierarchy among elders? The only hierarchy that is mentioned in Scripture is that the apostles had authority over the elders, and elders had authority over deacons. The same Greek word is used for both bishop and presbyter in the New Testament and was obviously referring to the same office in the apostolic writings. The elevation of the office of bishop above that of presbyter was a thing of gradual accomplishment. It was not recognized in church government until sometime between 70 A.D. and 120 A.D. Because of the way in which this happened, it seemed more rooted in selfish ambition on the part of some, rather than something the Holy Spirit initiated. It is understandable that many rejected it.

Emerging movements today use titles for the same function that range from "leading elder" to apostle. In some African-American movements, the term "bishop" is actually indicating more of an apostolic role than that which carried the biblical term for bishop. Biblically we cannot establish that any had extra local authority in the church except for apostles and prophets, or elders who sat on special councils with the apostles, such as we see in the council in Jerusalem. Outside of that special council, it seems that not any of these elders exercised extra local authority except as members of this special council.

DEACONS

The office of deacon was first instituted by the Jerusalem church in response to a need for those who could serve tables so that the apostles could devote themselves to the preaching of the word and prayer. The qualifications for deacons were nevertheless stringent, as we see recorded in I Timothy 3:8-13:

> **Deacons likewise *must be* men of dignity, not double-tongued, or addicted to much wine or fond of sordid gain,**
>
> ***but* holding to the mystery of the faith with a clear conscience.**

These men must also first be tested; then let them serve as deacons if they are beyond reproach.

Women *must* likewise *be* dignified, not malicious gossips, but temperate, faithful in all things.

Deacons must be husbands of only one wife, and good managers of their children and their own households.

For those who have served well as deacons obtain for themselves a high standing and great confidence in the faith that is in Christ Jesus.

This text is also viewed as proof for appointing women as deaconesses since it seems incongruous that this exhortation to women was found in the middle of these qualifications for deacons.

The Lord taught that as we do unto the least of His, we are doing unto Him (see Matthew 25:40), serving His people in such a capacity was a high honor in the early church. Many deacons were later promoted to the office of elder after proving their faithfulness as deacons. For many churches, serving as a deacon was a prerequisite for becoming an elder.

In the writings of the early church fathers, those who were the direct disciples of the disciples of the Lord such as the Epistle of Clement, who was considered to have been a disciple of the Apostle Paul, the remarkable devotion to humility in the early church was revealed. Being able to serve the Lord's household in even the most menial tasks was considered a privilege. In the early church, it was obviously taken seriously that the Lord's exhortation was true that the greatest of all was the servant of all.

SUMMARY

Many new movements are now sweeping across the church. They are coming with such life and vitality that they are forcing change by their very existence. The inability to accept change is a characteristic of those who have become old wineskins. The Lord is seeking to prepare wineskins that are perpetually flexible enough to embrace the new wine. The government of the church can be an aid or a hindrance to this.

The government of the New Testament church was the most innovative and flexible system of authority ever devised. As it matured, it became a blend of both hierarchy and democracy, promoting both liberty and order at the same time. Those who have been able to resist adding or taking away from it have a perfect framework which the Spirit of God can use. Yet it is also a framework for initiative and disciplinary measures that will always be needed from time to time.

The Lord could have been more specific in making a clear outline for church government in the Scriptures if that had been needed. What He did give us promotes dependence on the Holy Spirit. The Holy Spirit was not given just to give us guidance, but to be our Guide. Because He is our Guide, we must stay close to Him. This is essential for true spiritual leadership. It is Him with us—His anointing that gives us true spiritual authority. That was why it was so important for John the Baptist to see that it was the One upon whom the Holy Spirit rested who was the Christ. The Holy Spirit stayed with Jesus, and Jesus was constantly abiding in the Spirit. That should be our primary goal and is the qualification for true spiritual authority.

This is obviously crucial for true church life as it is intended to be. God does not anoint a position, but a person. We can have all of the positions in the church, but if the people are not anointed in them, they will be miserable failures at administrating the church. Likewise, we can have wrong positions, or even no positions, but if someone with the anointing comes, there will be authority. However, what we need to seek is both the right positions and the right people.

We only have true spiritual authority to the degree that we abide in the King and He abides in us. As He explained in John 15, we can only bear fruit if we abide in Him. Anointing is far more important than titles, education, and even experience. This is how the church was born and how it grew and stayed on track when it did. When unanointed people ascended to positions of authority in the church, she quickly ceased to be the church and became an institution and very quickly a tyrant, instead of a force for redemption, deliverance, and healing. We can build much with human effort, but we can never build the true church with it. Returning to true church government is fundamentally returning to the King.

CHAPTER FOURTEEN
WOMEN IN THE EARLY CHURCH

Women had a special and honored place in the early church life—indeed in the life of the Lord Himself when He walked the earth. The Lord does not have accidents, so we know it was no accident that it was actually a woman who was the first to see the resurrected Christ and the first to proclaim His resurrection, which was the basic commission of the apostolic ministry.

In the life of the first-century church, we see women involved in other firsts, such as being the first to be raised from the dead by one of the disciples and opening the door to the gospel in Asia. We will see as we study later church history that the place of women in the church, especially in leadership, has been in constant conflict and remains so to this day. Before continuing with the place that women had in the first-century church, I want to back up just a bit into the Old Testament to build a bridge to the New Testament.

THE GREATEST TEACHING MINISTRY

> **My son, observe the commandment of your father, and do not forsake *the teaching of your mother*;**
>
> **Bind them continually on your heart; tie them around your neck.**
>
> **When you walk about, they will guide you; when you sleep, they will watch over you; and when you awake, they will talk to you.**
>
> **For the commandment is a lamp, and the teaching is light; and reproofs for discipline are the way of life (Proverbs 6:20-23).**

Possibly the most important teaching ministry is also the most overlooked—the teaching ministry of mothers. As the above text from Proverbs states, we should observe the commandments of our fathers and not forsake the *teachings* of our mothers if we are to walk the path of wisdom.

Behaviorists have asserted that our basic character traits are set by the time we are four years old. A mother's teaching has its greatest impact on the child during these most formative years, which will have the greatest impact on the course of a person's life. Is there any ministry more important than helping our children get off to the best start possible? Could there be a ministry more worthy of honor and support than the ministry of being a mother? If we truly want to influence the future of the church and our world, this is where we must begin.

There is a popular cliché that says, "Behind every great man there is a woman." Usually we consider this to be the wife, and often it is, but the wife should be beside her husband, not behind him. Of those who accomplish great things, you will usually find a great mother who raised her child with strategy, vision, and the resolve to give her son or daughter all of the tools to accomplish his or her purpose in this life.

King Solomon was the most wise man to ever rule on earth. After writing the Book of Proverbs, which is the only book in the Bible devoted exclusively to wisdom, he concluded that this was **"the oracle which *his mother taught him"* (see Proverbs 31:1).** The wisest man who ever ruled on earth was taught his wisdom by his mother!

Solomon's mother knew that he was destined to be a king. It was a great responsibility to prepare the future king. Even so, our children have a greater calling than Solomon. They are called to rule and reign with Christ as kings and priests of a greater kingdom than Solomon's. Every mother of a Christian child is a true "queen mother" who deserves even more honor than any queen mother of a mere earthly kingdom. Solomon acknowledged this:

> **"Go forth, O daughters of Zion, and gaze on King Solomon with the crown with which *his mother has crowned him* on the day of his wedding, and on the day of his gladness of heart"** (Song of Solomon 3:11).

Solomon was the son of David, the great king of Israel. He was the heir to the throne because of his father, yet here he confessed that it was his mother who crowned him. This is the honor that has been given to mothers. As the Lord spoke through Moses, this is why we must do the following:

> **"Honor your father and your mother, that your days, may be prolonged in the land which the LORD your God gives you"** (Exodus 20:12).

In his letter to the Ephesians, Paul restates this commandment, ensuring that it would receive the same compliance by those under the New Covenant: **"Children, obey your parents in the Lord, for this is right. Honor your father and mother (which is the first commandment with a promise), that it may be well with you, and that you may live long on the earth"** (Ephesians 6:1-3).

For the entire time I have been a Christian, I have heard a great deal of honor given to spiritual fathers, but I have rarely heard any given to spiritual mothers. It seems that we are only complying with one-half of this commandment, which requires that we give honor to both fathers *and* mothers if our days are going to be prolonged. Could this be why very few moves of God keep moving for more than a few years, and then they begin to fall from their spiritual domain?

By the commandment, we are rewarded with longevity for honoring our parents. Those who do not honor their parents can be anything from indifferent and unthankful to dishonoring. In just a generation, we have seen the trend go rapidly from indifference to dishonoring. If this is not reversed in our country, we will soon be doomed, because the blessing of longevity will certainly be revoked.

The Law began with beckoning us to honor our parents with the hope of a great promise. It then proceeded to much more severe consequences. Exodus 21:15 declares, **"He who *strikes* his father or his mother shall surely be put to death."** Two verses later it is carried even further: **"He who *curses* his father or his mother shall surely be put to death" (verse 17).** Even though we are no longer under the Law for righteousness, the Law reflected God's standard of righteousness. The Lord cares very deeply about us honoring our fathers and mothers. Jesus Himself affirmed this in Matthew 15:3-4:

> **And He answered and said to them, "Why do you yourselves transgress the commandment of God for the sake of your tradition?**
>
> **"For God said, 'Honor your father and mother,' and, 'He who *speaks evil* of father or mother is to be put to death.'"**

Moses had said that he who curses his father or mother should be put to death, and Jesus interpreted "curses" as "speaking evil." The Lord did not just have men put to death out of harshness, but in order to remove the deadly spiritual viruses of iniquity from the camp so that others would not be infected. From the very beginning of His process of bringing redemption to men, when He first called Abraham, He established that the integrity of the family and the unfolding of His purpose from one generation to another was a fundamental vehicle through which redemption would be revealed, just as we see in Genesis 18:17-19:

The LORD said, "Shall I hide from Abraham what I am about to do,

since Abraham will surely become a great and mighty nation, and in him all the nations of the earth will be blessed?

"For I have chosen him, so that he may command his children and his household after him to keep the way of the LORD by doing righteousness and justice, so that the LORD may bring upon Abraham what He has spoken about him."

We see here that Abraham was chosen in order to command his children after him to keep the way of the Lord. It is noteworthy that we see here in relation to the man that he is to **"command his children."** This relates to what we read in Proverbs 6:20—that we are to keep the commandments of our fathers and the teachings of our mothers if we are to keep on the path of life.

SHOULD WOMEN TEACH IN THE CHURCH?

All of this brings up an important and controversial issue: Should women be allowed to teach in the church? First, let's look at the New Testament Scriptures that forbid this. The first is I Timothy 2:11-15:

A woman must quietly receive instruction with entire submissiveness.

But I do not allow a woman to teach or exercise authority over a man, but to remain quiet.

For it was Adam who was first created, and then Eve.

And it was not Adam who was deceived, but the woman being quite deceived, fell into transgression.

But women will be preserved through the bearing of children if they continue in faith and love and sanctity with self-restraint.

The second is in I Corinthians 14:34-35, which says,

The women are to keep silent in the churches; for they are not permitted to speak, but are to subject themselves, just as the Law also says.

If they desire to learn anything, let them ask their own husbands at home; for it is improper for a woman to speak in church.

These are clear and straightforward, so how could we possibly doubt that this was exactly what the apostle meant? The main reason why they have been challenged by sincere Bible believing Christians is that when they are taken literally, they stand in contradiction to other Scriptures which cannot be overlooked either.

A basic principle of biblical interpretation is found in Psalm 119:160: **"The sum of Your word is truth, and every one of Your righteous ordinances is everlasting."** If there is ever an apparent contradiction in Scripture, there is a reason for it. If we do not understand the reason, we do not base our doctrine on the one or two Scriptures that stand in seeming contradiction to the rest of the Bible, but we always go with the **"sum"** of the Word. Even so, this does not justify overlooking any Scripture. The tension between these is meant to drive us to a deeper understanding.

The first problem that we have when we take these Scriptures literally is that nowhere in the Law does it say that women are not permitted to speak. This seems to confirm what theologians have asserted, that Paul was quoting a letter or a report *from* the Corinthians concerning practices they had adopted and was then replying to them. Consider the next verses to be Paul's reply to the Corinthian practice of not allowing women to speak:

> **Was it from you that the word of God first went forth? Or has it come to you only?**
>
> **If anyone thinks he is a prophet or spiritual, let him recognize that the things which I write to you are the Lord's commandment.**
>
> **But if anyone does not recognize this he is not recognized.**
>
> **Therefore, my brethren, desire earnestly to prophesy, and do not forbid to speak in tongues.**
>
> **But all things must be done properly and in an orderly manner (I Corinthians 14:36-40).**

This may be the answer to Paul's statement in Corinthians but not the one in I Timothy. I have personally never heard an explanation for this one that satisfied me.

However, I do believe that there is an explanation because it is in contradiction to other Scriptures, and it violates Paul's own practice.

For example, Paul acknowledges in Romans that Priscilla and Aquila instructed Apollos, who became one of the greatest teachers in the first-century church. That Paul named Priscilla first, as the eminent one instructing Apollos, was such a blatant departure from the protocol of the times, in which the man was always named first, that it was considered to have been an intentional slap to those who would not allow women to teach in the church. At the end of this Letter to the Romans, when he listed those whom the church in Rome should greet, Priscilla was again named first, as if to verify his intention in this (see Romans 16:3).

Again, it is a basic hermeneutical principle that when one or two Scriptures are in conflict with many more Scriptures, or the entire weight of Scripture, we do not base doctrine on the one or two that stand in conflict with the rest. Whenever there are contradictions in Scripture, there are explanations for them, and we can be sure that the entire weight of Scripture will always be true and consistent.

It takes more bending of Scripture to hold to the doctrine that women should not be allowed to speak in church than it does to accept that they should. Even so, both positions do leave unanswered questions. Therefore, it seems wise that we not hold to either position dogmatically, but allow churches and movements to interpret this as they will, and not let it divide us if we have different opinions.

We must also esteem the Scriptures so that we would never just rationalize away a text that we do not agree with. If we are not satisfied, we should continue searching, but it is almost always a mistake to establish a doctrine of principle while still in conflict over an understanding.

There are many other ways in which both the Lord and the apostles honored and elevated the status of women in bold departure from the practice of the times. The Lord promised in Psalm 68:11, **"The Lord gives the command; the women who proclaim the good tidings are a great host."** In fulfillment of this, some of the greatest evangelists have been women.

A third major theological problem with women not being allowed to speak in the church is that there are women named as prophetesses in both the Old and New Testaments. This includes Miriam and Deborah in the Old Testament and Philip's daughters in the New Testament (see Acts 21:9). We are also told in the Books of Joel and Acts that when the Lord pours out His Spirit, our sons and daughters will prophesy. Would God give someone the gift of prophecy but not allow him or her to speak? Even in the Letter to the Corinthians, where it is stated that women should not be permitted to speak in church, just previous to this, Paul wrote that if a woman prophesies, her head should be covered. Again, how could she prophesy if she could not speak? So there is a very basic problem with translating this as Paul's own teaching.

A fourth problem that arises when we do not allow women to teach or speak in the church may be the most

WOMEN IN THE EARLY CHURCH

important of all. Could there be anything more dishonoring to our mothers than to tell them that they are not even allowed to speak in church? These mothers have probably been our most important teachers, who not only gave life to us, but nurtured and taught us from the beginning. The Lord thought mothers were so important for us to honor that it is the only commandment He gave with a promise attached to it—the promise of long life, which to most would be one of the greatest promises of all.

This is only a superficial address of an important issue. I have only tried to highlight some of the more basic principles that must be addressed. This is an important issue because it involves half of the citizens of the kingdom, half of the members of the body of Christ. Until women are allowed to function in the place in which they have been called, the body of Christ will be at best like a stroke victim that is half-paralyzed.

The church is called to be the light of the world, which implies that we must have the answers to the world's pressing problems. **"Where the Spirit of the Lord is, there is liberty"** (see II Corinthians 3:17), yet the church in our times has consistently not only failed to lead the great liberation movements of recent times, but has instead been their greatest enemies. This is understandable in some ways. When we fail to lead with sound biblical truth, the enemy will fill the vacuum with every form of perversion. Many leaders in the church have mistaken the nature of those who filled the vacuum as the nature of the whole movement. The primary reason why there is such perversion and extremes in the women's liberation movement is because the church did not take the lead in setting women free from the oppression they have been subject to. This movement should not be led by women, but by godly men who have the heart of God for His children!

We must rise up and preempt the enemy by taking the high ground on every important issue of our times. Even if we are starting late, as much of the church is doing in relation to women's liberation, it is not too late to seize the high ground of sound biblical truth, take our stand, and push the darkness back.

One of the great problems that we have in the church today is that there are many teachers, but not many fathers. Most of those who I have heard described as spiritual fathers are older men who have served faithfully for many years, but who in fact are not spiritual fathers, but just old teachers. A father is not just someone who is old, but one who reproduces. Most men become fathers when they are young, not old. A spiritual father is someone who reproduces his ministry and the grace that he has been given in others. Even so, for a man to become a father, a woman must be present. For a man to become a father, a woman must also become a mother. The reason why there are so few spiritual fathers in the church is because the women are not in their places.

We desperately need spiritual fathers, but we have just as much need for spiritual mothers, whom the Scriptures refer to as "mothers in Israel." We need to recognize and honor the women, who carry the seed of the Lord through intercession and then nurture the young with words of life and a constant vigilance. These spiritual mothers will be some of the best teachers of newborn believers, just as mothers are the best teachers of young children. This is not to negate the place of the men in this, but God made men and women to be different and divided the labor required to propagate the race. He also divided the labor required for the propagation of the church between men and women, and neither of us is going to arrive where we are called to be without the other.

The Lord does not want the differences between the sexes blurred; rather we must begin to esteem and honor the uniqueness of each. There is probably not a woman in the world who would not delight in being a woman if men became who God called them to be. If we are to attain His highest, we must comply more accurately with His plan. We will not have much lasting fruit in the church until we do.

In the natural realm, we also need to raise the esteem of motherhood to the great stature that it deserves— including the teaching that they have for us. When this happens, esteemed mothers will not continue to let their children pass through the fire, sacrificing them on the altars of selfish ambition or the false devotion to the deceptions of our consumer-driven culture. Our children don't need more things; they need more of us. To be a mother is one of the most unique, glorious, and fulfilling callings that one can have. We need to give the attention and the resources to this great ministry that it deserves.

Let us also esteem the women who cannot bear chil-dren in the natural, the widows, and those who do not feel called to be married. Many of these are the ones called to be the "mothers in Israel," or the spiritual mothers of the church, just as the Lord said in Isaiah 54:1-5:

> "Shout for joy, O barren one, you who have borne no child; break forth into joyful shouting and cry aloud, you who have not travailed; for the sons of the desolate one will be more numerous than the sons of the married woman," says the LORD.

> "Enlarge the place of your tent; stretch out the curtains of your dwellings, spare not; lengthen your cords and strengthen your pegs.

> "For you will spread abroad to the right and to the left. And your descendants will possess nations and resettle the desolate cities.

> "Fear not, for you will not be put to shame; neither feel humiliated, for you will not be disgraced; but you will forget the shame of your youth, and the reproach of your widowhood you will remember no more.

> "For your husband is your Maker, whose name is the LORD of hosts; and your Redeemer is the Holy One of Israel, who is called the God of all the earth."

When the world sees the godly women of the church in their God-given roles, being fulfilled to the uttermost because they are living what they were called to be, motherhood and womanhood will be esteemed as the glorious callings that they are. The Lord wants to display womanhood just as He wants to display His bride, the church. The church is a bride and is referred to in the feminine because that is a nature she is called to reveal. She will never be able to do that without women being in their place.

We also must understand that the bride is to be like "an army with banners." Armies tend to be masculine, and we will not be that until men are in their places. These may seem to be contradictory natures, but the male and female natures perfectly complement one another when they are right. When the Lord is finished with His church, the world will see in it the perfect glory of both the man and the woman. Men will look at the men in the church and say, "That is what I am called to be." Women will look at the women in the church and say, "That is what I am called to be."

The way I become one with my wife is not by making her a man. Our unity will only come when men are men and women are allowed to be women. Each must be allowed to be all that God created them to be. There would be no Jezebels if there were no Ahabs. Until both are free, neither can be free.

In the first-century church, women were given an unprecedented place of honor and esteem. The church was itself the very first true women's liberation movement. In it they were free, they taught, and they carried spiritual authority that was respected, and they did not have to become masculine to do this.

CHAPTER FIFTEEN

PERSECUTION AND PERSEVERANCE

In the previous chapters, we examined the basic message, lifestyle, and government of the first-century church. In this chapter, we will look at the effect that persecution had on the development of the Christian faith, since this was a considerable factor.

In the first century, Christianity was a supernatural experience. God is supernatural, and if we are going to experience God, it will be a supernatural experience. If we are going to walk with God, we must become comfortable with the supernatural. In the early church, the Lord Himself appeared to people at times. There were interchanges with angels to the degree that the church was exhorted to be careful how they treated strangers because they could be angels. The Lord was very close to His people, and the spiritual realm became familiar to believers. This did seem to make it easier for them to endure the almost continuous opposition, persecution, and afflictions.

The Scriptures make it clear that it will be the same at the end of the age, with both the supernatural characteristics of Christianity and the tribulations. Church leaders from the first century have understood this to be "the former and latter rains" (see Joel 2:23). We also see this in Acts 2:17-21, which Peter quoted from the Book of Joel:

"And it shall be in the last days," God says, "That I will pour forth of My Spirit upon all mankind; and your sons and your daughters shall prophesy, and your young men shall see visions, and your old men shall dream dreams;

"Even on My bondslaves, both men and women, I will in those days pour forth of My Spirit and they shall prophesy.

"And I will grant wonders in the sky above and signs on the earth below, blood, and fire, and vapor of smoke.

"The sun will be turned into darkness and the moon into blood, before the great and glorious day of the Lord shall come.

"And it shall be that everyone who calls on the name of the Lord will be saved."

Here we see that when the Lord pours out His Spirit, there will be prophecy, dreams, and visions. This is obviously increased in the last days because we are going to need it. Paul explained to the disciples, **"Through many tribulations we must enter the kingdom of God"** (see Acts 14:22). This was a proven truth in the first century. The more the church was afflicted, the more spiritual authority they experienced. Quickly they learned to be thankful for all such trials because they prepared them to be stewards of even greater power.

Everything about the young church seemed especially designed to draw wrath from all of the prevailing powers on the earth. The religious leaders of the time were threatened by any group that represented change or that they could not control. For the young church, they used almost any means to silence those they viewed as challenging their dominance, even to hiring false witnesses to bring charges against them, or turning them over to the hated Romans to be killed. Though the Jews had developed one of the most sophisticated systems of justice ever seen on the earth, they quickly abandoned it when dealing with Jesus or His followers.

Though usually given to an extraordinary due process, it seemed that at a whim they could exile Christians from the synagogue, which meant that people could not trade or relate to anyone in the community, driving them from their homes, their families, and their country. In this way, the religious oppression of first-century Israel could be as stifling as the political and military oppression of Rome. It was a difficult time to embrace any kind of new movement that was perceived to be a challenge to the status quo.

To call Jesus "Lord" also incited the Roman officials, who considered it an affront to the authority of the Emperor. This would ultimately release against the young church the most cruel persecutions yet experienced in the civilized world. Christians were marked as a special target for persecutions and afflictions, which could come at any time from any number of directions. Thus, to become a Christian also marked one as a part of a community whose courage was unprecedented. Never had a people arisen who were willing to suffer so much for the sake of their beliefs. The truth that they lived for was so great that they were also willing to die for it. For nearly three centuries, to believe in Jesus was to risk your life every day. The Lord Jesus had warned His disciples that this would be their lot, just as it was His:

"Behold, I send you out as sheep in the midst of wolves; so be shrewd as serpents and innocent as doves.

"But beware of men, for they will hand you over to the courts, and scourge you in their synagogues;

"and you will even be brought before governors and kings for My sake, as a testimony to them and to the Gentiles.

"But when they hand you over, do not worry about how or what you are to say; for it will be given you in that hour what you are to say.

"For it is not you who speak, but it is the Spirit of your Father who speaks in you.

"Brother will betray brother to death, and a father his child; and children will rise up against parents and cause them to be put to death.

"You will be hated by all because of My name, but it is the one who has endured to the end who will be saved.

"But whenever they persecute you in one city, flee to the next; for truly I say to you, you will not finish going through the cities of Israel until the Son of Man comes.

"A disciple is not above his teacher, nor a slave above his master.

"It is enough for the disciple that he become as his teacher, and the slave like his master. If they have called the head of the house Beelzebul, how much more will they malign the members of his household!

"Therefore do not fear them, for there is nothing covered that will not be revealed, or hidden that will not be known.

"What I tell you in the darkness, speak in the light; and what you hear whispered in your ear, proclaim upon the housetops.

"Do not fear those who kill the body but are unable to kill the soul; but rather fear Him who is able to destroy both soul and body in hell.

"Are not two sparrows sold for a cent? And yet not one of them will fall to the ground apart from your Father.

"But the very hairs of your head are all numbered.

"So do not fear; you are of more valuable than many sparrows.

"Therefore everyone who confesses Me before men, I will also confess him before My Father who is in heaven.

"But whoever denies Me before men, I will also deny him before My Father who is in heaven.

"Do not think that I came to bring peace on the earth; I did not come to bring peace, but a sword.

"For I came to set a man against his father, and a daughter against her mother, and a daughter-in-law against her mother-in-law;

and a man's enemies will be the members of his household.

"He who loves father or mother more than Me is not worthy of Me; and he who loves son or daughter more than Me is not worthy of Me.

"And he who does not take his cross and follow after Me is not worthy of Me.

"He who has found his life will lose it, and he who has lost his life for My sake will find it" (Matthew 10:16-39).

As the Book of Acts documents, the early church was born in persecution. With the exception of some brief respites, it grew and prospered in the midst of continual opposition. Diabolical rumors about Christians were devised and spread throughout the empire. The Christian "love-feasts" and celebrations of the Lord's Supper were declared to be a covering for the most hideous crimes. Not understanding the ritual symbolism of communion as partaking of the body and blood of Christ, the report was fostered that at such gatherings Christians would bind themselves into a criminal league by making a feast upon a slaughtered child and then give themselves up to the most shameless immoral indulgence.

The rumor that Christians were cannibals persisted for centuries. There was such revulsion at what was claimed that Christians practiced in private that soon every public calamity was attributed to Christians. The charge of cannibalism also justified to the Romans the feeding of Christians to wild beasts, which for a time became a sport in most major cities. Christians were hung on crosses, dipped in oil and burned, and some of these were even lit on fire to be used as street lights. Hideous tortures were devised as the Roman Emperor Nero unleashed the full power of the imperial sword in an attempt to destroy the young church.

To the great consternation of the Roman and religious officials of the time, the more they afflicted the young church, the more it grew and spread abroad. Every time a church was scattered, the people became like seed, and dozens of other congregations would sprout up. When one leader was killed, a dozen would arise to take his place. The Romans could defeat any army in the world, but they could not defeat the truth.

The more severe the persecution, the more grace was extended to the church by the Lord. Just as the first Christian martyr, Stephen, had beheld the glory of the Lord as he was being stoned so that he did not even seem to be aware of the mortal wounds that were being afflicted upon him, martyrs who were tortured by the Romans would experience such a grace that they did not even seem to feel the pain of their afflictions.

The peace and glory that would be reflected from them was so great that at times their torturers would be converted on the spot and choose to embrace the same kind of death for the sake of the truth found in Christ. Many who came to watch the Christians be devoured by lions were so stunned by their courage that they could find no peace until they too embraced faith in Christ. Nothing had ever been seen anywhere in the world like this. It defied any human explanation.

These persecutions against the church did not just last a few months, or even years, but for three centuries! The most intense persecution of all came during the last ten years of this period. On February 24, 303, an imperial decree was issued requiring the destruction of all Christian property and all copies of the Bible and reduced all Christians to the status of slaves. With their civil rights revoked, the entire populace of the empire was free to attack and afflict Christians in any way they desired. Their property was seized, their persons violated in every conceivable way, and multitudes were slaughtered. Yet the faith continued to spread and prevail, and the faithful grew even bolder in their witness.

Opposition can never hurt the truth; it can only help to purify it and make it stronger. During such times of persecution, there were probably no false conversions. Because leaders became special targets, those who accepted leadership positions were not motivated by selfish ambition but only out of a sincere love for the Lord and His people. Many of the petty issues that would cause division in the church in times of peace could find no place for producing discord in the persecuted church. Persecution was the fire that consumed the wood, hay, and stubble and purified the gold, silver, and precious stones.

Paul wrote to Timothy, his son in the faith: **"Indeed, all who desire to live godly in Christ Jesus will be persecuted" (II Timothy 3:12).** Jesus also said, **"Blessed are those who have been persecuted for the sake of righteousness, for theirs is the kingdom of heaven. Blessed are you when people insult you and persecute you, and falsely say all kinds of evil against you because of Me. Rejoice and be glad, for your reward in heaven is great; for in the same way they persecuted the prophets who were before you" (Matthew 5:10-12).** When viewing the procession of the church through history, it is apparent that persecution is the "normal" state of the truly faithful.

True Christianity has always been an affront and a threat to those who live by the ways of this present evil world, including professing Christians who have compromised with the ways of the world. This should never shock or discourage us; it should be expected. In fact, we should be more concerned when we are not being persecuted because it can be a sign that we are not really living in Christ Jesus and are therefore not a threat to the powers of darkness.

Persecution has a way of stripping away all of the facades and pretenses in order to reduce our faith and our lives to what we believe and hold essential. Those who really believe the truth of the gospel will not compromise it even if it means giving up their lives. The truth of the gospel *is* more important than this life. As a testimony to this, every one of the original twelve apostles died a martyr's death, with the possible exception of John, whose death was not recorded in history.

The following accounts were condensed from *Foxe's Book of Martyrs,* and the accounts of Jerome, Clement, and other early church fathers. These accounts are traditions that were passed down rather than eyewitness reports, but they are collaborated by so many that it is likely that they are at least relatively accurate.

THE MARTYRDOM OF THE APOSTLES

After the martyrdom of Stephen, James, the brother of John, suffered next. Clement wrote that when James was brought to the tribunal seat, the man who brought him there and was the cause of his trouble, as he saw James condemned to suffer death, was so moved by remorse that as he went to the execution, he confessed Christ himself so that they were led forth together. On the way, he asked James to forgive him for what he had done. James paused and then replied, "Peace be to you, brother," and kissed him. They were beheaded together in 36 A.D.

Thomas preached to the Parthians, Medes, Persians, Carmanians, Hyrcanians, Bactrians, and Magians. In Calamina, a city of India, he was slain with an arrow.

Simon, who was brother to Jude and to James the younger, and were the sons of Mary Cleophas and of Alpheus, became the Bishop of Jerusalem after James was crucified in a city of Egypt in the time of Trajan the emperor.

The Apostle Simon, called Cananeus and Zelotes, preached in Mauritania, in the country of Africa, and in Britain where he was crucified.

Mark, the evangelist and first Bishop of Alexandria, preached the gospel in Egypt, and he was drawn there with ropes, which pulled all of his joints out of their sockets. Then he was set on fire. This happened during the reign of Trajan.

Bartholomew is said also to have preached to the Indians and to have translated the Gospel of Matthew into their language. In Albinopolis, a city of greater Armenia, he was beaten with staves and then crucified and beheaded.

Andrew, the brother to Peter, was crucified by Aegeas, a Roman governor, in a city which is called Sebastopolis. Andrew, through his preaching, had brought so many to the faith of Christ that the governor came to the province to compel them to sacrifice to idols and renounce the faith. Andrew challenged Aegeas to his face, calling him to renounce his false gods and idols, declaring that the gods and idols of the Romans were not gods, but devils and the enemies of mankind. In a rage, the proconsul charged Andrew not to teach and preach such things any more, and if he did, he would be fastened to the cross with all speed. Andrew replied, "I would not have preached the honor and glory of the cross if I feared the death of the cross." Andrew was immediately condemned.

As Andrew was being taken to the place of his execution, seeing the cross being prepared in the distance, he cried out, "O cross, most welcome and long looked for! With a willing mind, joyfully and desirously, I come to you, being the scholar of Him which did hang on you, because I have always been your lover, and have coveted to embrace you."

Matthew, also called Levi, after he had converted to the faith Aethiopia and seemingly all of Egypt, Hircanus, their king, had him run through with a spear.

The Apostle Philip, after he had labored preaching the Word to some of the most barbarous nations of the time, was crucified and stoned in Hierapolis, a city of Phrygia.

James, the brother of the Lord, was esteemed by all of Jerusalem for his righteousness, being called "James the Just." When many of the chief men of the city believed, the leading Scribes and Pharisees ordered James to restrain the people from believing that Jesus was the Messiah. During the Passover, they carried him to a battlement on the temple from which he could address the crowds below. When James began to testify that Jesus was the Christ and was at that time sitting at the right hand of the Father, he was thrown from the top. He did not die immediately but struggled to his knees to pray for his persecutors. They rushed down and began to stone him. He continued his prayers, as Stephen had done before him, until he died.

Peter was preaching in Rome when he was entreated to flee the city because Nero sought to put him to death. As he was leaving through the gate, he saw a vision of the Lord coming to meet him. Falling to worship Him, Peter asked the Lord where He was going, and He responded that He had come to be crucified again. Peter understood that this meant it was his time to follow his Lord in death, and he returned to the city. When captured, Peter asked to be crucified upside down because he was not worthy to be crucified in the same manner as the Lord. His request was granted.

The Apostle Paul was also martyred by Nero. Nero sent two of his own esquires, Ferega and Parthemius, to Paul with the declaration of his death sentence. Paul prayed for them at their request and told them that they would believe and be baptized at his sepulcher. He was then taken out of the city and beheaded. The two esquires believed.

The persecution ceased under the Emperor Vespasian but began again under Domitian, the brother of Titus. In this persecution, the Apostle John was exiled to the island of Patmos. After the death of Domitian, John was released. He then went to Ephesus, where he remained until the time of Trajan. There he sat as an elder to the churches and wrote his Gospel. There are accounts of John's ministry continuing until he reached the age of one hundred. There are also several accounts of attempts being made by the Romans to kill John, but none of them were successful. One states that he was boiled in oil without effect before his exile to Patmos. Because there is no account of his death, it has caused some to wonder about the Lord's statement concerning John that was made to Peter:

> **So Peter seeing him said to Jesus, "Lord, and what about this man?"**
>
> **Jesus said to him, "If I want him to remain until I come, what is that to you? You follow Me!"**
>
> **Therefore, this saying went out among the brethren that that disciple would not die; yet Jesus did not say to him that he would not die, but only, "If I want him to remain until I come, what is that to you?" (John 21:21-23)**

THEY LOVED NOT THEIR LIVES UNTO DEATH

It was obviously a blow for the young church to see her leaders put to death. Even so, she did not waver but continued to grow stronger, and the gospel continued to spread. Seeing that killing the leaders could not stop Christianity, the Romans then turned to a general persecution against all who called on the name of the Lord.

In some cities, it was reported that thousands were put to death every day. At times, even the Roman officials were appalled at the slaughter, commenting that the Christians had done nothing worthy of such persecution. Seldom had one ever been found guilty of a crime or of doing any harm. The peace and patience with which they died, even when subject to the most cruel tortures, caused some of their persecutors to join themselves to the faith.

With intermissions, the persecution continued until the year 311, and in the most eastern districts, under Maximin, until 313. Its effect was to ultimately prove that Christianity was unconquerable.

Throughout much of the world today, Christians are under the continual threat of official, government-endorsed or led persecution. The nations where Christianity grew the fastest by percentage over the last ten years were the nations where the persecution was the greatest.

At the present time, Christianity is under assault from almost every direction, in almost every country, and is growing dramatically almost everywhere. In the 1990s, it was estimated to be growing at a rate of nearly 400,000 people per day! Christianity is growing three times faster than any other religion in the world and even faster than the population in some countries. It is now estimated that in the last ten years, one-third of all of the people who have ever come to Christ have embraced His salvation. It can be said of Christianity as it was said of Israel, "The more they afflicted them, the more they increased."

And not only this, but we also exult in our tribulations, knowing that tribulation brings about perseverance;

and perseverance, proven character; and proven character, hope;

and hope does not disappoint, because the love of God has been poured out within our hearts through the Holy Spirit who was given to us (Romans 5:3-5).

But remember the former days, when, after being enlightened, you endured a great conflict of sufferings,

partly by being made a public spectacle through reproaches and tribulations, and partly by becoming sharers with those who were so treated.

For you showed sympathy to the prisoners, and accepted joyfully the seizure of your property, knowing that you have for yourselves a better possession and a lasting one.

Therefore, do not throw away your confidence, which has a great reward.

For you have need of endurance, so that when you have done the will of God, you may receive what was promised.

For yet in a very little while, He who is coming will come, and will not delay.

But My righteous one shall live by faith; and if he shrinks back, My soul has no pleasure in him.

But we are not of those who shrink back to destruction, but of those who have faith to the preserving of the soul (Hebrews 10:32-39).

SUMMARY

This book is just a cursory overview of the first-century church, mostly from the perspective of important practices and doctrines, rather than events that we might normally equate with a history. However, we will cover many more of these details in later studies, as we will constantly be going back to the roots of the church in reference to the later doctrines and practices. This is just intended to be a most basic framework so we can now start building upon it.

The church was the most unique entity or movement ever to appear on the earth when it did, and it remains so even today. In many ways, in general, it drifted far from some of the roots that made it the most powerful force for good in its early history, and when it did drift, at times, it became a source of evil. We need to understand how this happened because it continues in almost each new spiritual generation. As those "gates of hell" are closed, we can expect the church to become the light and salt that she is called to be on earth and point the nations to prepare for the coming of the Lord and His kingdom.

The goal of this study is to help us perceive the unfolding plan of God, which included a prophesied departure from the way, a return, and a glorious conclusion. This is the greatest story ever told, and it becomes greater and greater as we approach the end of it. However, for it to have the intended ending, we must honor our fathers and mothers and learn the lessons of history so that a generation can arise that does not have to fall to the same mistakes. That generation will finish the highway that was commanded to be built to prepare the way for the Lord. Then He will come.

For Your **FREE** Subscription, call 1-800-542-0278,
or visit us online at www.MorningStarMinistries.org